Goodnight Sisters...

Nell McCafferty was born in Derry City in 1944. After taking a degree from Queen's University, Belfast, she travelled extensively on the Continent and in the middle east, finishing on a kibbutz in Israel. She returned to Derry in 1968 and joined the Derry Labour Party, the Civil Rights movement, and the dole. She moved to Dublin and joined *The Irish Times* in June 1970. She now lives in Dublin and works as a freelance journalist. A collection of her writings over fourteen years, *The Best of Nell,* became a best seller when published in 1983; and in 1985 she again reached the best sellers list with A Woman to Blame: *The Kerry Babies Case.*

First published in 1987 by
Attic Press
4 Upper Mount Street
Dublin 2

Reprinted 1990, 1994

British Library cataloguing in Publication Data
McCafferty, Nell
    Goodnight, Sisters: selected writings.
    1. Women - Ireland - Social conditions
    I. Title
    305.4'2'09417 HQ1600.3

    ISBN 1 85594 145 7

Nell McCafferty would like to thank Sue Russell, Noreen Green and Joel Conroy for helping her collate the material for this book.

Cover Design: Dynamo Design
Typesetting: 10/12 Galliard, by Typeform Ltd
Printing: Guernsey Press

Goodnight Sisters...

Nell McCafferty

Selected Writings. Volume Two

Attic Press, Dublin.

Contents

Introduction

I used to review the newspapers in a weekly RTE show called *The Women's Programme*. My function was that of feminist court jester, encouraging women to laugh at the silly things that were said and written about us. We were, as we well knew, whistling past the graveyard – this collection of articles records what was happening off-screen during that time, and since.

The nineteen eighties will go down in history as a lousy decade for Irishwomen. During what have become known as 'the amendment years', church and state fought for control of our bodies and our destiny. The Catholic Church won handily, and the Irish Constitution contains written prohibitions against abortion and divorce. Debate on these matters spilled over into all areas of the female condition, widening the scope for an unprecedented torrent of abuse and insult, the degrading marks of which are with us still.

The gulf between the lip service – paid by priest, politician and lay fundamentalist to their own notion of womanhood – and the reality of women's lives, is reflected in these articles. The eighties were as shocking as they were ineffably sad. The feminist vision was reduced to survival.

A previous collection, *The Best of Nell*, records the positively bouncy flavour of our yesterdays. I have included in this volume an article left out of that selection, because the drawn-out story of the Peace Women in the seventies shows that the agony of northern women is an unchanged and enduring feature of both decades.

Nell McCafferty, 14 August, 1987

The Holy Men

Next to Godliness

The Pope came out of the sky and descended into Ireland on Saturday 29 September 1979. It was a magnificently Messianic moment. The heavens had been cleared for it, and the earth brought to a standstill. All airports were closed, so that no man but John Paul could come down from above; all traffic had been banned in Dublin city so that pilgrims must walk to meet him; all workplaces had been closed, all over the country, that the people might be free to greet he who symbolized spiritual freedom.

No other place in the world had made such arrangements, but no other place in the world identified so strongly with the direct inheritor of the mantle of Jesus Christ. 'The Pope is infallible when he defines a doctrine, concerning faith or morals, to be held by the whole Church.' These are the words that echo and re-echo, unbidden in the mind, when all other words, learned off by heart, have faded away. Their meaning is awesome. The Pope knows what God thinks, and says what God means, and the Pope is absolutely right. When the Pope speaks, God is speaking.

The Pope, when we were first taught those words, was a figure unreal as the man in the moon. He lived far, far away. We would never meet him, nor did we expect to meet him, no more than we ever expected to meet God on this earth.

Then a man landed on the moon.

And going to Rome was as common, more common given the cost of a holiday in the West, than going to Killarney.

But still the aura of magic remained.

Men might go to the moon, and all of us might go to Italy, but the Pope would remain immobile and unmoved, there in the Vatican, deep in the panting heart of Rome. Also, an Irishman would never be Pope. So we kept our distance and he kept his and the Godliness of it all was right and proper and seemly.

No wonder the nation came to a halt when he came over here. I mean to say, Jesus Mary and Joseph, who would have thought it, or wrought to think of it. I was in Blackrock when his plane appeared in the sky, suspended over Howth. As it came drifting closer, hearts stopped with the wonder of it all. 'There's the Pope,' we shouted, laughing and disbelieving and proud as a chosen people could be.

In the Phoenix Park a million people gathered, happy and carefree and innocent of evil intent as a bunch of babies. Goodwill and good cheer emanated like sunshine, and the sun did indeed shine from a cloudless sky. The ushers and orderlies and security men were redundant. A joyfully corralled nation behaved as if blessed, and thought itself blessed, and *was* blessed when he stood atop his Popemobile and was driven up and down and through our serried ranks, so that no one was far from him, and the Irish people felt as close to God as it was possible to be.

He looked the part: handsome, virile, gentle, happy and gorgeously dressed, in white silk, satin and glowing gems. We never heard a word he said, but no matter, for the words had been with us since birth, and the ritual of the Mass an automatic reflex genuflection.

We went home content, we Irish who had seen the Pope, and next day we switched on the television to watch his progress through Limerick, Galway, Knock, and Drogheda and those were the days when the earth turned on its axis and the world as we knew it fell completely apart.

He who was infallible spoke rubbish. Black, he said, was white. Faith fled like snow off a ditch. The Emperor was left with only the clothes he stood in. No one has referred to him since but his words will never be forgotten. John Paul the Second single-handily destroyed the authority of the Roman Catholic church which had held unchallenged domination over the minds and hearts of the Irish nation since Patrick plucked the shamrock.

'Tu es Petrus
Et super hanc petram
Aedificado ecclesiam meam . . .

Thou art Peter, and upon this rock I will build my church and the gates of hell shall not prevail against it. And I will give to you the keys of the kingdom of heaven. Feed my lambs. Feed my sheep.'

This guy blew the sheep off the rock and out of the water.

Women, he said in Limerick, should return to the kitchen sink. Paid work outside the home was bad for them, for their offspring and for their husbands. Contraception was no good either. This was the equivalent of telling children they shouldn't have pocket money or buy Smarties. Shortly afterwards, Mr. Limerick

himself, Dessie O'Malley, founded a new political party and defin-
ed Durex, in the Dail, as the apex of democracy.

Murder is murder, John Paul declared confidently in Drogheda,
looking north where he had not the nerve to go. 'On bended knee
I ask you to stop', he asked the Provos, and everybody in posses-
sion of a telly could see that he was sitting on a chair as he said
this, and there was no way, however much the nation still clung
to the faint hope that somehow, somewhere he would show
himself infallible, that the viewer could be persuaded that a Pope
sitting on a chair was also on bended knee.

Shortly afterwards the people of Fermanagh elected Bobby
Sands, Officer Commanding the IRA in Maze prison, as their
Sinn Fein member of parliament at Westminster; Kieran Doherty,
also of the IRA, was elected TD for Cavan; and Paddy Agnew,
also of the IRA, was elected TD for Louth. Cardinal O'Fiach's explanation that people saw their elected Sinn Fein representatives
as helpful in matters such as gardening – God help me, I'm on the
floor laughing as I write this – was seen as so much ecclesiastical
shamrock.

The Pope's visit, said Eoghan Harris at the time, would set
Ireland back sociologically ten years for about three weeks. He
was wrong. John Paul brought us right smack into the twentieth
century, and with only fourteen years to go until we reach the
twenty-first there is every indication that the people will come of
secular age right on the button. He untied the Gordian knot of
church and state and personally exposed the fallacy of infallibility,
leaving the holy men in frocks in tatters, for which let us give
thanks. God bless the Pope.

In Dublin, 17 April 1986.

Altar Girls

A man wrote to the *Evening Herald* asking why there were altar boys and no altar girls. A woman from Ballyfermot wrote in published reply that the parishioners of Our Lady of the Assumption were pleased to announce that altar girls are out there 'working in conjunction with the boys, assisting at Mass, weddings and funerals, and they are doing a very fine job. We are proud of them.'

The woman gave her address and telephone number.

She is sorry now that she did.

She told *In Dublin* that the priest, whom she refused to name, had told her that she shouldn't have written the letter. She had been given to understand that she had done something wrong, but she wasn't sure what it was, since it was all right to have altar girls. Well, nearly. It was nearly all right, as far as she could tell, but something was wrong, though she wasn't sure what and she wished to God she'd never written to the *Herald*. The Catholic Press and Information Service was much less frightened about queries from *In Dublin*, but cheerfully said that an article about altar girls would blow the gaffe and probably bring a stop to the whole thing.

Altar girls, it would appear, have been slipping in beyond the Irish rails, under the benign eye of some priests, beyond the malevolent sight of Rome. A clerical source has explained the whole thing.

'I wish to remain anonymous', he said. 'No, I'm not afraid, but there are times when a priest looks like an eejit standing over Canon Law, and I refuse to be a printed eejit on this occasion, a grown man trying to make out there's a difference between little girls and little boys when it comes to ringing a bell.'

Canon Law 230 of the new – ie progressive – Canon Code states that 'lay-men' may serve as 'lectors and acolytes'. That is to say, they can read the lesson and ring the bells beyond the altar rails. The term 'lay-men' is calculated and specific. It is not a generic term meaning men and women. Where men and women are concerned, Canon Law specifies 'lay-people'. Theological lawyers did not come down in the last shower.

Canon Law 230, therefore, is quite definite. It is talking about jobs for the boys.

However, the same said Canon Law 230 allows females to perform the same said tasks 'by grace and goodwill rather than by right'. That is to say, women and girls might sometimes venture beyond the rails to read the lesson and ring the bells, providing the priest is full of goodwill and they don't get the idea that this is going to be in any way a permanent thing. He's just giving them a break.

It came to pass that in Washington, USA, altar girls served at masses, weddings and funerals so often that the idea got abroad that altar boys were no more, and altar persons was an idea whose time had come. Rome got wind of this. Eight months ago Rome ordered Washington to banish girls from the altar. An order came from the most powerful Christian city in the world to the most powerful capitalist city in the world that pre-pubescent females should be told that they were inferior to pre-pubescent males. Otherwise the world as we know it might collapse in pagan immoral disorder.

'This is a fact. I feel an eejit telling you, but this is a fact', the source told *In Dublin*.

The order, and its consequences, was flashed and relayed around the world in the highest Catholic theological journals.

'Ah well, theology, I don't know much about that, you'd need to ask someone else about that' says a priest in Clondalkin who has for the past twelve months been presiding over the sight of altar persons youthfully ringing joyous bells upon the altar where he says Mass.

'I suppose though', he added sadly 'if that's the law, this is the end of it. I didn't know there was anything wrong in it. It all looked very nice to me.' The same priest (who also doesn't wish to be named) does have his own standards though. Last year his girls and boys helped him at Confirmation ceremonies. This year he has ordered altar boys only for Confirmation, and altar girls only for First Communion.

'It wouldn't look good for them to be mixed at a big public function' he explained. 'It looks better if it's one or the other.' He added that anyway girls wouldn't be able to carry the cross at Confirmation ceremonies. He busted his sides laughing at the suggestion that he provide lighter crosses for the Confirmation ceremonies. 'You women are never satisfied' he chortled.

The priest in Clondalkin, the priest at Ballyfermot who wouldn't return *In Dublin* phone calls, the priest at the Catholic Information Centre, the source, and the woman who wrote to the *Evening Herald*, are all of one mind on one thing - now that *In Dublin* has publicised the fact that altar persons serve on two altars in Ireland, Rome will come down on them like a ton of bricks.

No moves will be made to banish adult female readers who appear on every altar in the country. They know from life long experience of everything ranging from paid work to birth control that they have got by on a wing and a prayer. Whatever they have they hold not by right, but by the grace and goodwill of the men who control their existence.

Little girls though, are blissfully unaware of the mark of Cain. They carry within their small innocent unformed untrammelled female bodies the very seeds of destruction of the male based Roman Catholic Church. Canon Law 230 anticipates this. Canon Law 230 was issued around the same time as Chuck Berry's 'Ding a Ling'.

In Dublin, 19 April, 1984.

No Sex Please — We're Irish

Bishop Eamon Casey laughed his leg off when Eamon Kelly told a joke on *Saturday Night Live*. So did Eamon. So did the audience. No doubt, a lot of viewers laughed too. It was one of the saddest jokes ever told against ourselves on television.

A traveller was offered the hospitality of the house, said Mr Kelly. This included an overnight stay. There being only one bed, the wife slept nearest the wall, the husband in the middle, and the traveller on the outside. When the husband got up to go to the toilet, the wife said to the traveller 'Now's your chance'. The traveller rose like a man to the occasion and devoured a freshly baked cake that he'd yearned for all night.

Laugh? I nearly cried at this televised and applauded display of crippled sexuality. Mr Kelly displayed all the manly qualities of a broth of a boy, daring to tell a joke about marriage and a double bed in front of a prince of the Catholic Church. The bishop showed himself as one of the lads by his gleeful attention. Two grown men, meeting man to man on television, before the nation, to chat about sex – was anything more natural or homely or enjoyable?

The joke was, of course, that a man would prefer to eat cake than make love with a woman. The point of a really good joke is that it flirts with the truth. And the bishop roared with laughter as the truth sunk home – no sex please, we're Irish. All's well in the double beds of the nation – a man could pack a dozen of his pals in there and be sure that nothing would happen. The woman who longs for love – why else would she issue an invitation to the traveller – must settle for crumbs. There is an unconscious element of spite in this, as the lads laugh at how they can have their cake and eat it too. The bishop and Eamon Kelly cannot be dismissed as men past their prime, clinging raucously to outdated notions of human sexuality. The plaint of 'The Midnight Court', when women railed against an absence of healthy lust in their menfolk, is as sure today as it was when first uttered in the seventeenth century. One of the best looking men in the country (a prominent journalist to boot) boasts that he would prefer a plate of mashed potatoes and a glass of buttermilk to a night with a woman.

A standard joke in Irish male repertoire is that a man would crawl over the bodies of a dozen naked women to get to a pint of Guinness.

Repetition of such jokes causes gales of laughter, as witnessed on *Saturday Night Live,* when the bishop and Eamon Kelly fell about in mirth when a sexual variation was recounted. These men are laughing at female frustration and male inability to relieve it. They invite us to laugh at the sexual cripples we have become.

If we laugh hard enough, the psychology goes, we'll forget the underlying pain. The men can get a further chortle out of the fact that the woman made the cake which proved her undoing. There's one in the eye for the adulteresses of this fine, upstanding moral country.

Given the occasion that was in it, the question is this: why didn't Eamon Kelly tell us a joke about the bishop and the actress? There are a million of them around. Laugh? I would have cheered.

Kerry's Eye, 13-19 November 1986.

'I'm as Sexual as . . .'

'I'm as sexual as anybody else and there are a thousand ways to express that sexuality'. The person who said that is not Mae West. The words were not uttered by Sappho. Nope, it wasn't Oscar Wilde. Wrong, it wasn't Madonna. The Virgin Mary? You must be joking. No, no, no, St Joseph never let the words pass his lips. Listen here now, leave Oliver Flanagan and Charlie Haughey out of the discussion.

Yes, of course, you know a dozen people who've said the very words to you; it's par for the course; promises, promises, promises. We should be so lucky.

Give up?

Wanna try three more guesses?

You'll never guess.

The person who said those words was Bishop Eamonn Casey in a *Hot Press* interview. He, you will remember, is the man who sold a hospital on condition that the doctors who bought it from him did not perform sterilisations. He is as sexual as anybody else and knows a thousand ways to express that sexuality.

He isn't a bit shy about it either. He gave a few examples of his personal theological Kama Sutra. For married couples he recommends 'shaking hands'. He was quite explicit about it, no humming and hawing and substituting four letter words as gross euphemisms for coupling. 'Shaking hands', he came right out with it, is a sexual act.

Bishops, as we know, seldom shake hands.

They hold out one bejewelled finger and ask for a kiss on the ring.

Phew!

There are other steps to earthly heaven.

He recommends 'an embrace, putting up with each other, listening, being silent, being tender'.

So far, we've performed seven of the one thousand acts he recommends. That leaves nine hundred and ninety three to go. At which point – orgasm? Ejaculation? Perhaps. Consummation? Certainly not. At that point the bishop withdraws. 'There's a thousand ways in which you express sexuality *other than sexual union*' he says. This is odd. The Catholic Church is quite explicit about consummation being an integral feature of the sexual act. Some time ago, in England, the Church refused to solemnise the marriage of a paraplegic man and an active woman, on the grounds that the man would be unable to complete the sacramental act. Completion, said the Church, involved the penetration of the vagina by the penis and ejaculation into the vagina. The couple had a thousand ways of their own of giving sexual pleasure, but they admitted that they couldn't achieve number one thousand and one.

No consummation, no sexual union, said the Church.

Foreplay, the Church dismissed the couple's bag of tricks.

Nothing wrong with foreplay, of course.

Very good for you.

Shaking hands is not an earth shattering way to begin, but we have to take account of culture, locality, custom and tradition. The South Sea Islanders start by rubbing noses, after all. Can't see that catching on here. Can't picture Bishop Casey and Barry Desmond rubbing noses, particularly not after the hospital deal. Can't imagine the implications, anyhow. Can't imagine what to think, tell you the truth, next time I see a picture of some bishop shaking somebody's hand. What, I shall ask myself, do we have here.

Nope.

Bishop Casey hasn't quite got the hang of sexuality There's a lot more to it than shaking hands, saying nothing, and looking tender. A lot more.

It's rather more vigorous than he imagines.

It hardly bears imagining, to tell the truth.

In fact, it's quite ridiculous, the shapes people throw when they get down to it. There are few positions more ridiculous – to look at – than the positions people adopt when they get together. Limbs everywhere. Orifices gaping. Mucus pouring out and in. Sweat flying. Sheets wrecked. Animals and insects fleeing the scene when the going gets rough. Noise? My dear, the evacuation of Dunkirk in World War Two was an intellectual discussion compared to it. Once in a while, of course, there's silence. Usually afterwards. It's called exhaustion.

You don't get exhausted shaking hands.

I mean to say, tell the truth, when's the last time you saw an exhausted bishop?

Nope, he hasn't quite got it right yet.

Furtive Lechery

In Lahinch, County Clare, on a recent hot August night, women gathered outside a pub door, seeking fresh air. Other revellers, students of the annual Merriman Summer School, remained inside pursuing the hares raised during a week's discussion of 'The Priests and the People'. The theme had seemed particularly apt; the school was founded in 1968 with the intention of commemorating Brian Merriman, whose banned, bawdy seventeenth century poem 'The Midnight Court' contained a lusty appeal from frustrated women to priests, urging them to do what the elderly celibate laymen of Ireland would not do.

That particular hare had not been raised during this week.

On this one night, however, outside that pub, the women, for no reason at all, spontaneously began to confess to each other. They confessed quietly lest the neighbours should hear. Every single one of them had been interfered with, mentally or physically, by a priest.

Next morning, at a seminar, quiet, angry reference was made to the 'furtive lechery' of priests, but the remark was not taken up and no one sought details. That was to be expected. When a few women, some years ago, spoke quietly and publicly about wife battering, the details were so shocking and the inferences to be drawn about men within marriage were so disturbing, that the phenomenon was quickly labelled 'Scream quietly or the neighbours will hear'.

On this night then, in Lahinch, the women confessed quietly to each other their experiences of priests.

Here are some of the details.

Mary, when eleven years of age, was brought during the school 'retreat' into a room to confess to the priest. They were alone. She knelt before him. He pressed her head into his lap. He asked her if she had ever had sex with animals. He told her never to believe that it was right to 'do it' with boys when she was bleeding, because she could just as easily get pregnant then.

She was eleven and did not know what he was talking about, or what he could be feeling with her head pressed into his lap, but as she grew older and learned about life, the memory came back to haunt and disturb her.

Martha, when aged fifteen, was confessing during another school retreat, and was also alone with the priest in a room. She admitted to French kissing but could not find words to capture the details required. 'Was it like this?', asked the priest, putting his arm around her and his tongue into her mouth.

Those are the speakable details.

What was remarkable about that group of women, five in all, and comparative strangers to each other, was not the details of their stories, but the commonality of their experience. Each one of them had been interfered with, physically or mentally, by a priest. Some were luckier than others. They were adult women when it happened, and more able to cope.

The question arises though: how common is the experience to Catholic women? It is a difficult question to pose, on many levels. The subject is taboo. Its implications are disturbing. Credibility is hard to establish, because one is mainly dealing with little girls.

Little girls who complain about fathers are shied away from. Little girls who complain about Holy Fathers would find people steering a wide berth around them.

This columnist can complain of nothing more substantial than the priest who picked up her book on Freud, opened it at a chapter headed 'Sex', and admonished her that it was dirt which should not be read without permission from a bishop. When you're twenty-one though, in search of a teaching job in that priest's diocese, and the job is in his gift, you can be made to feel very dirty about sex. Your mind can be interfered with in a massive way if you're in a dependent position.

How widespread is this molestation of girls and women by priests? Confess quietly or the neighbours will hear, but confess; for if it is widespread it is damnable, destructive and ought to be stopped.

In Dublin, 6 September, 1984.

Little Richard

The connection between Little Richard and Irish Catholic Bishops may at first seem tenuous, even obscure, especially to anyone born since 1960. Not to worry.

All the bishops were born before 1960, and lay people, it may safely be said, did not come down in the last shower as regards matters sexual.

Even the bishops recognise that. People, they have more or less indicated, were born the way they were born, and it can't be helped. Which brings me directly to Little Richard.

Sometime in the sixties he took part in a movie called *The Girl Can't Help It*. This movie featured Jayne Mansfield, a woman with a forty-two inch bust. As she strolled across the screen, Little Richard screamed in his inimitable fashion 'The girl can't help it, she was born to be'. Lest that message escape some folk, Richard repeated the line, so that we staggered youthfully from the movies grunting 'The girl can't help it, she was born to be, yeah, the girl can't help it, she was born to be'.

Rock 'n' Roll, you gave me the best years of my life.

Truly.

Anyway, the bishops, Little Richard, and I are now in tune.

Take the bishops' recent pastoral on love and sex, for example, remembering as you do, that Little Richard is now a proclaimed practising homosexual pastor, in the *Christian* tradition. In other words, he ain't no muslim, man, nor hindu, nor pagan. He's a rock and rolling homosexual christian, sister.

The boy just can't help it.

No problem, say the Irish Catholic Bishops, in their pastoral letter. 'It is not christian to depise homosexuals and exclude them from society'.

Homosexuals, OK, say the elderly lads.

Furthermore, they say, 'homosexual tendencies can be innate and irreversible'.

A wop bop a loo-laa, a wop boom bam.

The boy can't help it. Need more be said?

Alas, yes.

The bishop was not born who did not have more to say. These lads can't help it. Pondering that which is irreversible, the bishops engaged in an intellectual *pas de deux* that is familiar to graffiti connoiseurs.

To be or not to be.

To do is to be.

Do-be-do-be-do-be-do.

Or, as the bishops formally put it, homosexual tendencies 'can cause drives and temptations which are difficult to control or resist'. This being so, 'some homosexual actions may lack the full freedom and deliberateness necessary to constitute grave sin'.

The boy can't help it!

Neither can the girl!

'This is not a mortaller'.

We were meant to be.

'Each case', the bishops stressed, 'must be judged individually and compassionately'.

Could anyone ask for more?

Did any reasonable human being, ever, on this earth, ask to be judged other than individually and compassionately? Come back, Little Richard, all is remembered. *Christ, you know it's getting easy.*

Out Magazine, No. 3 April 1985.

Men Only

The Anglican and Roman Catholic Churches are moving rapidly along the road to unity, but the holy men of both faiths have come up against a major stumbling block — women.

The Anglicans have allowed the odd woman to become a minister in faraway places in the United States, Canada and New Zealand, and are considering the ordination of female ministers in England.

In Ireland, their women can't even become deacons. As for the Catholic Church — forget it. No dame need even think of applying.

The Archbishop of Canterbury, chief of the Anglican chiefs, seems quite envious about the way the Vatican head man has kept women off the altar, and has hit upon what he clearly believes to be a very good reason for throwing women off his.

'I have always been cautious about concentration on the ordination of women at the expense of christian unity.

If it wasn't for women, in short, these guys would have been united long ago.

We were brought up on such fairy-tales, of course. First we were taught that if it weren't for Eve, Adam and company would still be in the garden of Eden.

That story about her offering him a bite of the apple is a thinly disguised allegory about sex — she wanted a cuddle, he succumbed, and next thing they were flung out on their ears.

The Catholic Church has been in a fit about sex ever since. Their priests are ordered to maintain strict celibacy, and the holy men insist that a virgin became a mother without any involvement with a man.

The Anglicans have tip-toed around that one, but they're putting the boots on now that the prospect of international power has been dangled before them. The Rev. Runcie has spelled it out clearly — if women are the price, he'll sell them out, no expense spared.

His manoeuvring on the matter is outrageous. Having recognised that the Yanks, Canadians and New Zealanders are unlikely to defrock their women ministers he has come up with logic worthy of the Pope: female priests, perhaps, in foreign parts, but female bishops never, anywhere. The Yanks, you see, are considering promoting one of their women to bishop.

A woman bishop, he says 'raises questions about the unity of the Anglican Church, and not just the theology of the ministry'. What does he mean by that?

If anyone can explain to me what he means by that I shall personally cast a personated vote for the Rev. Ian Paisley at the next election. A minister is a minister, and a bishop is a minister who gets to wear a nicer frock.

Perhaps his slip is showing, and he merely means that it is all right to have women workers, but not women bosses.

Perhaps not.

Who can make sense of these guys?

The Pope at least is intelligible when he says no women at any rank in his organisation. It doesn't make sense, but at least his meaning is clear. Out, out, out he says, and he won't even countenance altar girls ringing his bell, though he's so desperate to keep up the head-count of Catholics around the world (numbers are dwindling) that he maintained a perfectly straight face when the bare-breasted straw-skirted women of Papua New Guinea danced before him and proclaimed themselves faithful.

Breasts are in, bishops are out, as regards the female of the species.

Is there anything more ridiculous, I ask you, than a bunch of holy men in frocks saying women shouldn't wear frocks? Personally, I think Eve should have made Adam eat a lemon.

Sunday News, 20 April 1986.

Women Too?

The men in charge of An Post decided last week to issue a set of stamps celebrating the contribution of women to Irish society. They threw a party, provided lots of wine and food, invited women along, and sat back to receive congratulations. The poor sods. Whatever made them think that Irishwomen would be content to receive a lick and a thump on the face and vicarious travel on the front of an envelope?

Gemma Hussey, Minister for Social Welfare, was having none of it. She went straight to the heart of the matter, the position of women within the Catholic Church. After five years and two referenda, during which the church helped define the current position of the female sex – subservient – she chose to make a comeback.

Her point was devastatingly simple. The church plays a large part in the social life of Ireland. The church sets standards for the people. The church's standard for women is that of second class citizen. Women have as much hope of taking power in the church as blacks have of taking power in the white government of South Africa. No black may seeks position in government. No woman need apply for a job in the church hierarchy. The priesthood is reserved for men only.

Her comments struck a raw nerve, and reaction has ranged from outrage to support. It looks as though we are about to enter a period of serious debate about the role of women in religious organisations. When we do, the men of religion will find that they have much to answer for, and much that is unanswerable. For starters, they might try to justify some of the religious quotations reproduced in the feminist bible *Sisterhood is Powerful,* which was published in 1970, and is still valid today.

All of the following quotes are still uttered worldwide, and are considered integral to the practice of religion:

I thank thee, O Lord, that thou hast not created me a woman — Daily Orthodox Jewish Prayer (for a male).

In childhood a woman must be subject to her Father; in youth, to her husband; when her husband is dead, to her sons. A woman must never be free of subjugation — The Hindu Code of Manu, V.

If thy wife does not obey thee at a signal and a glance, separate from her — Sirach 25:26.

Creator of the heavens and the earth, He has given you wives from among yourselves to multiply you, and cattle male and female. Nothing can be compared with him — Holy Koran of Islam.

How can he be clean that is born of a woman? — Job 4:4.

And the rib, which the Lord God had taken from man, made he a woman and brought her unto the man. And Adam said 'This is now bone of my bone, and flesh of my flesh; she shall be called Woman, because she was taken out of Man' — Genesis 2:22-23.

Let the woman learn in silence with all subjection. I suffer not a woman to usurp authority over men, but to be in silence — St Paul.

Wives, submit yourselves to your husbands . . . for the husband is the head of the wife, even as Christ is the head of the Church — Ephesians 5:23-24.

God Created Adam, Lord of all living creatures, but Eve spoiled it all — Martin Luther.

All witchcraft comes from carnal lust, which is in women insatiable — Kramer and Sprenger, Inquisitors of the Catholic Church.

Woman as a person enjoys a dignity equal with men, but she was given different tasks by God and by Nature which perfect and complete the work entrusted to men — Pope John XXIII.

This last quote means, among other things, that men get to serve on the altar, and women get to clean the altar up afterwards. All the quotes indicate clearly that within organised religion women are held to be innately inferior. Gemma Hussey has decided to stamp such notions out. She launched the renewed battle for independence at the GPO in Dublin. This woman has a cheeky sense of style.

Kerry's Eye, 21-27 August 1986.

Silent Night

Silent night, my eye. Are they trying to tell me that Mary went through labour on a stable floor, surrounded by animals, with not a groan out of her? Childbirth isn't like that. Admittedly you'd think twice about letting out a roar with a great big ox's hoof right beside your ear – didn't Joseph organise things well, typical bloody man – but she must have let out the odd exasperated sigh. She must have said something like 'Jaysus, Joseph, you're a bollix'. She could hardly be condemned for that. The woman was in labour, and in trouble, and anyone who's ever come within an ass's roar of a maternity ward knows that the language can be choice.

All is calm, my elbow.

She probably said 'Joseph, will you stop filling in those bloody census forms, push the ox over against the wall, and let's clear a bit of space around here, for Christ's sake, can't you see I'm flat on my back and getting trampled?'

Shepherds quake at the sight, my foot. A star twinkled and they went into a panic. Can you imagine what it was like back there in the stable, when the waters broke, the blood flowed, and the baby fought its way out of the mother's womb. Must have frightened the life out of the ox, a baby squealing like that. Joseph probably fainted. And the churches ask me to sympathise with a bunch of men with nothing better to do than round up the sheep.

Heavenly hosts sing Alleluiah. I can just picture Mary. Alleluia*aaagghhhhh*. There's no way Phil Coulter can get them out of this one. It must have been blue bloody murder in there. The last thing she needed was a bunch of angels stringing their harps. Typical, innit? She's lying there exhausted, trying to breastfeed, and Joseph decides to have a party.

Glory to the newborn king, aye surely. Admittedly the woman was probably dead proud of her child, but a little bit of congratulations was in order for her, surely? It's hardly beyond their brains to devise one lousy tune, for the day that was in it, in honour of the mother?

Not at all. All I hear about are red-nosed reindeer, two front teeth, scarlet ribbons, and little drummer boys going rup a bup bum. Spare a tear, too, for the poor man coming into sight gathering winter fuel. He gets the sticks, Mary gets the cow's breath. Have any of these guys ever smelt a cow's breath? She must have been throwing up.

As for the Three Wise Men. What's so wise about them? They got lost, they arrived late, and they landed in without so much as a bottle of milk between them. Gold, frankincense and myrrh, that's what they brought her, gold, frankincense and myrrh. She needed myrrh like she needed a hole in the head. 'Here's some myrrh, Mary' – how she kept a polite tongue in her head, I do not know. 'Oh, yes, myrrh, look, Joseph, this nice man has brought some myrrh. Stick it over there beside the frankin what-chamaycallit'.

Bet the police were called when she tried to cash the gold in the pawn-shop. 'Honestly, officer, I was lying flat on me back, in me stable, when in walked this king and he gave me all this gold . . . Joseph? Joseph? Jaysus, Joseph, they're taking me away'.

Away in a manger, no crib for a bed, the little Lord Jesus laid down his wee head . . . where do they think Mary laid hers? Up the road in the Bethlehem Shelbourne, no trade union labour wanted? She was lying there too, you know. You can put a baby down anywhere and it wouldn't know the difference; all it does is sleep, shit and feed off its mammy. What about her? A fully grown adult, probably needing stitches, surrounded by straw and shit. Baby's shit, ox shit, sheep shit, and myrrh. Her head must have been bursting.

Oh come all ye faithful, joyful and triumphant. Hey Joseph, would ye ever tell the faithful to fuck off. A person can't get a wink of sleep round here. Animals, shepherds, kings, angels, and now here come the bleedin' bloody faithful. Does nobody realise that I'm lying flat on me back in a kip. Get me outta here, Joseph, or I'll call this kid Fred.

In Dublin, November 1986.

No Pope Here

If women keep on attacking him this jet-setting Pope is going to end up like the Shah of Iran, flying round in ever widening circles looking for sanctuary. The word has clearly gone around that John Paul is bad for business. Holland has coped with hippies, South Moluccans, an embezzling Prince, sex and cyclists and drug pushers, and still attracted tourists, and then along comes your man and out into the streets with batons the hitherto invisible Dutch police had to go.

It is not difficult to imagine the scenario in some foreign country a few weeks hence. The phone rings in Sweden. Marcinkus is on the line from the Vatican murmuring that the Pope needs a foreign travel fix. 'The Man is getting restless', says the Vatican banker. 'Eff off', say the Swedes.

No Pope Here is the slogan of the future.

The rot set in after John Paul left Ireland. Hardly had he set foot in America than a nun waltzed up to the microphone and let him have an earful of criticism. That is called, in political parlance, an idea whose time has come. It has spread like wildfire.

Among the women.

The Catholic men have fought him on many fronts and accepted expulsion and silencing in reply. Men are hung up on the rules. Like Kevin Moran, when they get sent off, they walk right back to the dug-outs.

Catholic women are different. They're not used to playing by the rules, because they've never been allowed to play. Thus when the Pope sent word to a Dutch convent that he'd be staying for four nights, bed and breakfast, they sent word back that he could stay one night, the normal courtesy available to any traveller, and no more. 'We're in mufti now', the nuns said. 'You wouldn't like it. We wouldn't like you'.

Poor Popie Jopie.

The woman I liked best — as usual the papers didn't think it worth their while to print her name — was the one who went along with the rules right up to the moment she was standing in front of him. She wrote out her speech, they vetted her speech, she took the stand with her speech, and then tore it up. 'Pope' she said (I give a rough translation, my metier being French),

'Pope, you've got it all wrong about sex. This is the way things are . . .'

He had to sit there, trapped in the television lights and a live broadcast, and listen to it. The interpreter sitting by his side and whispering in his ear was blushing like a Flanders poppy.

Belgium, they said, would be better. So he crossed the border and went into Belgium. The woman chosen to address him then was the Walloon equivalent of the president of the ICA. 'Holy Father', she began. A man can't be addressed more respectfully than that by a woman. 'Holy Father', she said, 'we don't mind bearing and rearing children, but when that's done, which doesn't take long, we have certain ideas about a further career'.

So saying, she walked away from the kitchen sink, in behind the altar rails, and diffidently suggested that there was no reason why a woman shouldn't, at around the age of fifty, think about becoming Pope.

The guy is reported to be back in the Vatican now, poring over a world atlas, looking for a place where women know their place. Bishop Newman of Limerick has given a hint. The followers of Islam, he said recently, are most obedient. Catholics, he said, could well take a leaf out of their book. An Irish judge caught the hint and reminded Eileen Flynn that women are stoned to death over there. Does the Pope read the Irish papers?

Is the ayatollah about to get a phone call?

God bless Catholic women. They make the earth shake under his feet.

In Dublin, 30 May 1985.

After the Amendments

As Far as Practicable . . .

● *'I am being asked to decide about a non-existent unborn child and a non-existent pregnant woman',* said Justice Hamilton. Nell McCafferty sat through the four days of argument, supposition, hypothesis, high drama and farce as SPUC's attempt to prevent the Well Woman Centre and Open Line Counselling advising women on how to procure abortions in Britain came before the President of the High Court.

Liam Hamilton, President of the High Court, went to Mass on Monday morning, with all the other luminaries of the Irish legal system. The mass marked the opening of the courts for business, after the summer holidays. Next day, Tuesday, 7 October, a hand-written sheet, affixed like a fly-poster to the door of Court Number One, in the Four Courts, proclaimed Mr Hamilton's business. The Society for the Protection of Unborn Children (SPUC) versus the clinics would be heard before him, starting at two in the afternoon. Roll up, roll up.

They did, and the court was packed and proceedings began at two precisely. The high drama was punctuated almost at once by an element of farce. As a lawyer for the Well Woman Clinic mentioned the Treaty of Rome, invoked the European Court of Human Rights, and reached for a weighty book, an elderly barrister stepped out of the crowd and asked the Justice to consider another case entirely. He had been queuing since before two, said the barrister. Had Dickie Rock interrupted the opening scene of *Hamlet,* on first night in the Abbey, to sing *Candy Store,* the effect could not have been more deflating. Justice Hamilton did not conceal his annoyance. 'You need only look around you to see what I'm facing', he voiced his mood.

The barrister persisted, and the audience availed of the disruption to look around at each other. The women of the clinics sat in one row and the women of SPUC sat in another. The benches were filled with supporters of both sides, some wearing flowers in their lapels, others wearing the notorious gold-plated reproductions of foetal feet. These symbols apart, the physical difference between the two sides was cruelly obvious. The clinic women and their supporters were vibrantly youthful, clearly of child-bearing age. The SPUC women and their colleagues were markedly older, their child-bearing days long gone. The comparison invited night-marish stereo-typing, and muttered comments over the next four days of the case, as people streamed out for coffee or lunch, confirmed that the bitterly wounding years of the 1981-83 abortion campaigns have left an unwomanly legacy.

'They couldn't provide enough tissue between them to make one uterus', an onlooker attacked the SPUC women. 'The clinics encourage whoredom in Kimmage', said an acid observer of Open Line Director Ruth Riddick's red hair, red lipstick and fingernails, red handbag and red shoes. Woman's compassion for woman, betrayed when a member of SPUC walked into the clinics and falsely pleaded an unwanted pregnancy, had reached the end of its tether in the courtroom. There was no noticeable wave of sympathy for Bernadette Bonar, the anti-abortion and anti-divorce leader of the Responsible Society. Her husband died just days before the case began. Her face was pale with sadness. She slept while the lawyers spoke.

The real legacy of those years when the nation tore itself asunder was made abundantly clear in the High Court as Justice Hamilton and his assembled men of law briskly agreed that if one thing was certain, it was this: nobody knows what the Eighth Amendment to the Constitution means. The words that racked the people now had the lawyers on the rack, comfortable though it was at one thousand pounds per man per day, and they freely exchanged expressions of sympathy with each other and with the Justice before whom they elegantly tortured their brains as they pondered those words: *'The state acknowledges the right to life of the unborn, and, with due regard to the equal right to life of the mother, guarantees in its laws to respect, and as far as practicable by its laws to defend and vindicate that right'.*

The state, in the form of Dail politicans, had huffed and puffed about that guarantee, all sound and fury signifying nothing, the lawyers assured each other. The politicians had not passed one single law since then that would guarantee the right to life of either mother or child. All the legal men had to guide them was the 1861 Offences Against the Person Act, outlawing abortion. As regards new laws 'the short answer is no . . .', said Hugh Flaherty for SPUC. From a legal point of view, the Eighth Amendment had not 'advanced the situation any more than already existed', added Anthony Kennedy, also for SPUC.

However, he pointed out, if the politicans had not helped the un-born, they had at least been prevented, through the Amendment, from harming them. It was agreed that the clinics had not broken the law of 1861. They were not performing abortions. They were doing no wrong in that respect, but the people, said SPUC, had a right to defend the unborn against what the clinics actually were doing. The Director of Public Prosecutions could find no reason or evidence on which to charge them with criminal activity but 'where there is a right, there is a remedy', said Mr Kennedy, and the remedy sought by SPUC was a court order forbidding the clinics to give information about abortion.

SPUC held that by giving out such information the clinics failed to vindicate the right to life of the unborn; and that by distributing pamphlets which actively encouraged women to come there for pregnancy counselling, the clinics were actively procuring and assisting pregnant women in Ireland to travel abroad for abortion, or receive advice on abortion. SPUC also contended that by their activities, the clinics were conspiring to corrupt public morals. Tony Kennedy cited examples of corrup-tion that were morally repugnant to the Irish people – attempts to entice young girls under fifteen to leave the father's house and engage in fornication; attempts to introduce women into pro-stitution; and now this. Mr Hugh O'Flaherty for SPUC said the option of having an abortion carried out should not be mention-ed, debated or advised on.

The emphasis on the right to life of the unborn brought several quiet interruptions from Justice Hamilton. 'Does the question of the legal right to life of the mother come in . . .' he asked. This question worried and nagged him, and he threw it first to one side, then to the other. 'Of course,' said SPUC, 'the mother has the right to life as well. But leaving that aside –'. The Justice would not let any of them leave it aside. He did not see, he said, how he could consider one aspect of the amendment without tak-ing the other aspect into consideration. If both the mother and the unborn child had rights, and a decision had to be made about which of them had the superior right, 'Who is to make that deci-sion?' he wanted to know. 'It is extremely difficult', confessed SPUC. 'We don't know who . . .' However, said Hugh O'Flaher-ty, abortion could not under any circumstances be performed in the Republic, and the question, he inferred, was academic.

The Justice did not think it was academic at all. 'The Constitutional rights of the unborn are being interfered with within this jurisdiction. In many cases, pregnancies are being terminated to protect the health of the mother'. Does it not happen frequently, he badgered SPUC? It wasn't spoken about, 'because everybody's turned a blind eye to it'.

The court did not speak about it in detail, either. The lawyers turned their eyes to other aspects of the case. Two days later, the Justice returned to the problem. 'What are the circumstances in which a pregnancy can be terminated?' he asked Tony Kennedy. 'That is the seemingly insoluble dilemma of the Eighth Amendment', responded Mr. Kennedy.

By the fourth and final day, SPUC had come up with an answer of sorts. No evidence had been presented to the court that pregnancies were terminated in Ireland, said Mr O'Flaherty. The Justice was assuming medical knowledge. 'I am assuming medical practice', said the Justice. 'There's certainly no evidence, but I don't live in an ivory tower'. 'If we are going to get into the larger area of cultural practice', said Mr O'Flaherty, then SPUC reserved the right to call medical evidence. At the back of the court sat a doctor, newly arrived, who campaigned for SPUC during the anti-amendment years.

Neither the Justice nor Mr O'Flaherty ventured into the larger area. In the corridors outside, the public speculated about the cultural practices and ivory towers and blind eyes alluded to. It was assumed that Justice Hamilton had in mind the termination of ectopic pregnancies, which occur regularly in the Republic. An ectopic pregnancy means that the fertilised egg is stuck in the fallopian tube, and cannot fall down into the womb. If allowed to grow in the tube the egg would become a foetus, then an unborn child which would burst itself, the tube and the woman asunder. In Catholic hospitals here, doctors may remove the tube containing the fertilised egg. Culturally and theologically speaking, the Church argues that this operation does not constitute an abortion. The primary intent and effect is the removal of a diseased organ, the fallopian tube. The secondary and unintentional effect is the termination of the pregnancy.

In England, this is called an abortion.

A woman with an ectopic pregnancy is entitled to information about her condition of course, and advice on how to deal with it within the Republic. The Health Act specifically states that information about abortion is legally available and may be given, provided a licence to give such information is sought from the Minister. Irish hospitals have not taken up the invitation to apply for such a licence. The formal implications of having one are that certain cultural procedures might be deemed to be abortifacient.

Justice Hamilton approached the matter in another way. He asked if there could be lawful discussion on the question of whether a pregnancy could be terminated, having regard to the Eighth Amendment.

'I think there can', admitted Tony Kennedy for SPUC. 'I think so, too' said the Justice. However, he pointed out, Mr Kennedy's SPUC colleague, Hugh O'Flaherty had said no. Mr Kennedy argued that Mr O'Flaherty meant there could be no discussion where there was intent to have an abortion, regardless of circumstances.

The Clinic lawyers argued that the clinics neither counselled abortion or referred women to England for abortion. The clinics merely told pregnant women of all the options open to them: a pregnant woman could have her child and keep it, or have it fostered, or have it adopted, or have the pregnancy terminated. Such information, said Peter Maguire for Well Woman, did not bring the pregnant woman 'any closer to abortion than when she came to the clinic. Indeed, when she leaves the clinic she may decide not to have an abortion'. The clinics could not refer women to England for abortions, as alleged by SPUC. They could only refer them to English clinics 'for further pregnancy counselling', and the English clinics might decide, after consultation with one such woman that she was not entitled to have her pregnancy terminated, or she might decide herself not to have an abortion. It followed logically from such procedures that Irish clinics were not operating as abortion referral centres. They were merely imparting information about services available elsewhere in the EEC, and David Butler argued for the Well Woman that under the Treaty of Rome a person had an absolute right to go to another country and avail of the services which were legally obtainable there. He said that such services must be remunerative, and abortion service in England had an element of remuneration – the woman must pay.

Mr Butler's emphasis on remuneration raised many of the

ghosts of the anti-amendment years, and the court proceedings then took a strange turn. Far from arguing, as SPUC once did, that family planning activists were part of a multinational concern to make money and profit out of women's condition, James O'Reilly rose in court, on behalf of SPUC, to assert that the clinics were not in the money making business, and that the right to avail of services elsewhere did not therefore apply. The clinics provided a service confined to Dublin, he said. If they wanted to plead rights under European Community Law, they would have to show that they carried on business in another state, and this they clearly did not do. There was nothing commercial about abortion, he said.

The lawyers embarked on a tour of the commercial services of Europe, reaching for books and citing cases. Pregnant women and unborn children faded into the background as they talked of a German Communist who was refused a post graduate grant, a Duchess whose Church of Scientology activity led to her expulsion from Britain, an Italian who failed to report that he had hired an au pair, and a Dutchman who fought for the right to help cyclists go faster in other countries by accompanying them on a motorcycle.

Nearer home, SPUC insisted that under the Constitution a mother who did not have enough to live on could sue the state for extra maintenance. 'The State shall ensure that no mother shall be obliged by economic necessity to engage in labour to the detriment of her duties in the home'. Supposing, Justice Hamilton mused along this utopian path, a woman went out to her job, found that her children were being neglected as a result, found that when she returned to full-time home duties that she was flat broke, supposing . . .

The nature of the suppositions took on a back-to-the-future aura. In the absence of an actual mother, or an actual unborn child, warned the lawyers for Open Line, the Justice was being asked to make a decision about 'the unknown unborn and an unknown pregnant woman.'

More than that, added the Justice. He was being asked to decide about a 'non-existent unborn child, and a non-existent pregnant woman'.

No mother was speaking for herself in court, said Paul Carney. And the unborn can't speak for itself, said the Justice. The Justice was listening, in effect, to three limited companies said Mr Carney. A binding court decision would mean that 'a future mother cannot distinguish herself from a previous mother'.

Frank Clarke, on behalf of Open Line, stressed the 'extra-terrestrial' nature of legal abortion in England. If the Justice were to strike down a woman's right to information about abortion, the consequences would be as bleak as they were entirely imprac-ticable. 'If it must be so, it must be so', he said, and sketched what it would be. A woman could be restrained from travelling to England, if the court were satisfied that she intended to have an abortion there. A woman could be prevented from permanently emigrating, if it could be shown that she contemplated abortion in the course of her emigration to God knows where. If a foreign magazine, available here, published an article that mentioned the option of abortion, the editor, publisher, directors and journalist could be jailed. Referring obliquely to certain cultural practices, he said that 'having regard to the moral climate in Ireland, it might not be possible for a mother to obtain an abortion here, because it is a matter of common sense and public notoriety that many hospitals have views on what can be done'. If there were cir-cumstances in which abortion could be legally carried out, however, and the rights of the mother, mentioned in the Con-stitution, implied that there were, 'there must be circumstances when she is entitled to information and advice on whether she qualifies.'

What circumstances? What information? 'Even if such advice were to avoid back street abortion or to avoid inducing by dangerous means?' the Justice asked himself and the lawyers.

The advice would be not to have an abortion, said SPUC.

Women were entitled to information, said the clinics.

'Information which leads to what?' the Justice brought himself back to the unborn who could not speak.

'Are you asking me to substitute myself for the legislature?', the Justice asked SPUC.

'Where parliament fears to trend, it is not for the courts to rush in', cautioned David Butler of Well Woman.

In the absence of a clear guideline, through laws laid down by the politicians, Anthony Kennedy sought to soothe the raw nerves of the judiciary, a Justice had to do what a Justice had to do. 'As invidious as your role is, it is imposed on you by your

Constitutional obligations to do the best you can, in as imaginative, inventive and creative way as you can do'. His oath of office, obliging him to uphold the Constitution and laws 'does not leave a lot of room for invention, imagination and genius', the Justice said when he had pondered the advice.

Well Woman lawyer David Butler urged him to have regard for the 'Olympian' clarity of judgements handed down in European Community Law. Tony Kennedy exhorted him instead to be 'Delphic'. The court, he said, was on 'the horns of a dilemma' in this case. If the legislature omitted to clarify a matter, the Justice said, it was of course open to the court to remedy the omission. 'Nobody wants to do it', he said, almost sadly, but he could see that there was a Constitutional obligation on the judiciary. However, he had 'extreme doubt as to whether I am the arbiter of public morals'.

In many respects, SPUC consoled him, the Eighth Amendment to the Constitution was 'unclear'.

'In many respects?' echoed the Justice sardonically. He said he would give his decision at the end of November. Besides the many unclear aspects of the Eighth, there were six major points to consider. He thanked the 'gentlemen', rose and was gone.

The gentlemen wondered what the six points could be. The women went off to await the verdict. A dozen of them could have been pregnant, of course, and none of the gentlemen would have known.

In Practice

At a public meeting next Monday night in Liberty Hall, Dublin, feminists will consider how best now to help women with troubled pregnancies.

As of that morning, barring an exceptional legal loophole, the Open Line Pregnancy Counselling Centre will close its doors forever and the Well Woman Centre will never again offer a counselling service to pregnant women in need.

'It would be unfair to charge them money for advice and information, when that advice can no longer include the option of abortion,' says a spokeswoman for Well Woman. 'Most of the women who have come to us in the past to talk about their pregnancies have had abortion on their minds and it would be cruel to delude them into thinking that maybe the address of a British clinic will slip out of the side of a counsellor's mouth.'

Official figures show that 4,000 Irishwomen went to England to terminate their pregnancies last year. Unofficially, the figure is put at around ten thousand. Given that the Well Woman and Open Line centres between them only counselled 1,000 Irishwomen last year, not all of whom opted for abortion, it is obvious that the vast majority of women travelling to Britain for pregnancy termination have found their own ways and means of obtaining the necessary information.

In practical terms, therefore, the court order obtained by the Society for the Protection of the Unborn Child (SPUC), which prohibits the two centres from giving information on abortion, is useless. An entire network of relatives and friends, built up through generations of emigration to Britain, has ensured the free flow of information between these islands.

It is not even necessary to operate by word of mouth, and nudge and wink and whisper. The addresses of three British pregnancy advisory services, where abortions may be obtained, are printed in the *Irishwomen's Guidebook and Diary,* which is on sale in bookshops throughout Ireland. Ten thousand copies of the diary, published by the feminist imprint, Attic Press, have been sold since Christmas.

The direct dialling code to Liverpool and London has been helpfully included. All a woman needs to do to obtain an appointment with the British clinics is consult the diary, put her shillings in a coinbox, and phone straight through from Sligo, Lisdoonvarna or the most remote village on the Irish western seaboard.

British women's magazines, which sell by the several thousand every week in this country, and are available in every corner shop from Bantry to Bailieboro, contain advertisements and articles which constitute a veritable guide through the maze of the fertility rite, from virginity to contraception to conception to pregnancy testing at home, to termination over there.

A full-page ad in *Woman's World*, for example, offers a do-it-yourself pregnancy test called Discover Colour. 'You simply compare the two beads to see the result . . . and as the test uses the same modern technology as hospitals and clinics, you know you're getting the most accurate result available . . . (the test) can be carried out on the very day your period is due.'

A woman with an overdue period need then merely consult *Cosmopolitan* magazine, which carries every month two advertisements which declare 'Abortion advice and help. Immediate appointments'.

Such magazines are bought and read avidly and faithfully and regularly in Irish households which contain a cross section of women ranging from members of SPUC to members of the Defend the Clinics Campaign.

To compound the irony, and formalize the Irish solution to an Irish problem, libraries throughout the country stock another Attic Press imprint, *Woman to Woman*, a health book written by Ann Roper of Well Woman, which contains a detailed question and answer chapter on everything a woman might want to know about abortion procedures, including the addresses and telephone numbers of British clinics. The book was launched on the *Late Late Show* last winter, and Ms Roper subsequently spoke on several RTE radio programmes.

Even the British telephone directory – which lists clinic numbers – has been mentioned as a transgressor of Irish law, come Monday.

In the light of all this, and in the absence of censorship, next Monday's meeting in Liberty Hall might seem irrelevant. The Irish clinics might have shut down their pregnancy counselling services, but the abortion trail to Britain is as clearly signposted as the route to the Four Courts, where Mr. Justice Hamilton will formally publish his decision on Monday morning.

In effect, the meeting in Liberty Hall will mark the formal launch of a campaign to legalise abortion in Ireland. Having first established the principle of the right to know, to which the meeting will address itself, it is logical that one day the campaigners will address themselves to the right to choose termination of pregnancy in this country.

By successfully applying the ultimate sanction of silence in the privacy of a clinic, SPUC have, ironically, forced Irish feminists to come together publicly and speak out.

Irish Press, 8 January 1987.

No Divorce

The Divorce Referendum was launched in government buildings by men of substance. Alimony payments would have posed no problem to the Taoiseach, Garret FitzGerald, or the Tanaiste Dick Spring, or the Minister for Justice, Alan Dukes. Money did not enter the minds of the mainly male journalists who questioned them at the press conference. The lads had a grand talk altogether about law, the Roman Catholic Church, love and the five-year limit. The roomful of career men did not take into account at all the fact that marriage is virtually the only career open to adult females, that it is an unpaid career, and that redundancy would pose severe problems for them.

Within days of launching that referendum, the same men were clutching their wallets and offering women welfare. A divorced woman could claim the same benefits as an unmarried mother, or a deserted wife, they said. The descriptions fell like insults on wounded hearts. Unmarried mother, deserted wife, divorced woman *versus* the Taoiseach, the Tanaiste and the Minister. Never have the job divisions between women and men in this country been so baldly and cruelly laid on the line.

The final degradation

Most adult women in this country are married. Most married women engage in labour inside the home. A vote for divorce was a vote for the sack and legalised poverty. 'It's like asking turkeys to vote for Christmas', said Fine Gael TD Alice Glenn, completing the deluge of degradation that poured on the heads of Irish women when the meaning of marriage was explored. Turkeys depend on their owners for food, shelter and life itself.

The women of this country, who voted overwhelmingly in 1983 to defend the lives of the unborn, voted in similar numbers in 1986 to defend their own. Divorce was rejected.

Love and sex had nothing to do with it. That is the single most appalling result of the referendum. Women voted to stay in marriages that are devoid of tenderness, trust, companionship and passion because they depend on the money husbands pay for their services in the kitchen. We voted to stay with the clenched fist and marital rape because the alternative is hunger and poverty. We took the soup.

What else could we do in a country where children are totally dependent on full-time mothering, and mothers function as unpaid dependent wives? It was open to Messrs FitzGerald, Spring and Dukes on that night in May, when they proposed divorce, to offer a proper package that would have included an increased children's allowance, vigorous enforcement of equal pay and enhanced job prospects for women. A nod in the direction of creche facilities for civil servant females, who work for the government these men run, would have indicated an understanding of the difficulties that a divorced mother could face. It did not occur to them. They still have not understood that child-care and money are essential features of a free woman's life. This is all the more inexplicable given that these men could not themselves function – would not function – unless they were paid for their jobs and had someone to take care of their children for them.

These were facts as obvious as the nose on the face that pro-divorce campaigners refused to admit. Of course the rate of marital termination would have increased, however temporarily, had divorce been introduced. Of course male wages could not have been adequately split to support two households. Of course the divorced woman would have been plunged into poverty.

In exchange, she would have gained peace of mind, the dignity of independence, and the chance to love again, if such were her wish. These, however, are qualities unknown to us – love, sex, and independence formed no integral part of the first marriage contract, why should they be available second time round? There will be no divorce in this country until such things are expected of relationships between men and women.

We could, of course, have brought in divorce to please the Northern Protestants and further the aim of a United Ireland. Since the Northern Protestant is perceived to be a Northern Unionist, and Unionists are demonstrably reactionary – so reactionary and anti-democratic that the right of self-government was taken from them by Garret FitzGerald and Margaret Thatcher – the only surprise is that the anti-divorce vote was not higher. Turkeys have a hard enough time without bringing a Unionist farmer into the premises.

All that being said, it is probable that divorce will be introduced into Ireland before the twenty-first century. More women than ever are now working outside the home, and the numbers go inexorably up. The woman with money in her purse can afford room for love in her heart. When that day comes, the unloving male will be stuffed.

WPA Journal No. 22

A Life in Limbo

On the night before the Irish voted massively against divorce, a representative from Debrett went on BBC television, which is available to most Irish viewers. The Englishman smoothly outlined the etiquette for seating divorced parents at the Royal wedding. The mother and her second husband would sit on one side of the aisle, the father and his second wife would sit on the other. The children of the first marriage would sit . . .

And the whole world would watch.

Jaysus.

This is how we do things across the channel: A man confirms that his marriage is finally over. His father's face sets in concrete and his mother clutches her breast. She knew, says the mother, the day her son set off for his wedding that it would not work. There was no telling him that, of course. He was over twenty-one. Deep sorrow, dismay and sadness seep into his clan. There is a hint of terror. He is a Catholic. The future looms blank, black and silent, in face of that fact.

The man does the decent thing. He leaves the village.

Everybody accepts the public story that he has gone in search of work. His wife retains status. The man comes back for the First Communion and Confirmation of his children. He does not stay long and people know not to ask why. He knows not to talk about the distant town where he now lives. He is a man without a past or a future.

In his middle age the man falls seriously ill. His mother knows not to ring the house where he lives. She does not want to hear a female voice. She cannot go to the hospital where he is lying. She would be unable to confront the fact that the woman visitor on the other side of the bed has a relationship with him.

The name for this relationship is stark, brutal, insulting and immutable in a country where 95 per cent of the population subscribes to the Roman Catholic faith. Adultery. Rather than use this term, because we are as human as everybody else and know that nobody went down the aisle of the church in the bright days of youth meaning harm to anybody else, we solve the dilemma by neither confronting it nor thinking of it. It is consigned to the unspeakable, the unthinkable, to the theological limbo between heaven and hell, where God alone will judge.

Limbo used to be known as the place where little babies went if they died suddenly, before baptism, or pagans went whom we were unable to reach. Limbo lulls, limbo soothes – if our human judgement on the babies and the pagans seemed harsh, we knew at the back of our tortured minds that God would look after them eventually, and bring them to heaven, because God is omnipotent and ultimately loving and can solve riddles.

As a theological concept, limbo has been quietly dropped, but the lay memory of a religiously untutored race is strong, and we retain limbo in our thoughts as an earthly place of hope for our separated brethren, those brothers and sisters whom we know and love and had to put outside the parish pale. Please, God, look after them for us.

So the mother picks up the phone and asks one of her daughters to go and visit her son and see that he is all right. There is no need to explain why it has to be done this way, and no desire to have it spelt out. We cannot argue with the revealed truth mediated by the priests, and we cannot bear to look closely at the way we behave in consequence.

Too much sacrifice has made a stone of our hearts, said the poet Yeats. We were reared in school and at home on the sacrifices made to keep the faith alive through the dreadful times of the penal laws, when the English who ruled Ireland decreed that no Catholic could own a horse worth more than five pounds, and the priests risked death to say forbidden Mass in the ditch.

The daughter goes to the far away town and meets her seriously ill brother and the woman who is worried sick about him, keeping watch by his bedside, and the children who call him Daddy. The little innocent cheerful children are delighted to meet their new Aunt. God forgive her, and God will, she plays at happy family with them.

This was no time, around that sick bed, to raise the bitter memories of the poverty he left behind, the other children he seldom saw and had little chance to see anyway, because we sent him into exile. Later, his sister and his mother speak, sparingly, about him, and the truth of his other life forces itself in under the weight of the ultimate question: what if he had died? In which town would he have been buried, who would have gathered around the graveside, who would have spoken to whom, or handle the worst fate of all, that of making the introductions? So many children, looking like him, not knowing each other, or the terms for each other. 'This is his wife, this is his . . .' Other woman?

Jaysus, Mister Debrett.

The mother and daughter lightened the pall with black jokes. Cremate him. Scatter the ashes from Belfast to Bantry. Stick two empty wee boxes in two graves at opposite ends of the country. No one would be the wiser and there'd be enough brothers and sisters to make up a crowd at both funerals.

Cremation is a growing fashion whose time has come in Ireland. There is one crematorium on each side of the border.

The brother recovers and rings his mother. He wants his second family acknowledged. He has nearly died and he longs for his mammy. He's lonely in exile and he longs to come home occasionally, like the grown man he is, and share the details of his life and family, just like everybody else. Which family, asks his mother, fiercely loyal to the only one she knows.

She has her own problems to contend with. She is elderly now, and knows how close her own death is. It is time to review her life, the family she reared, and her relationship with her God. She had thought long and deeply about the consequences of the last constitutional referendum when the country voted massively against abortion. Babies unborn are God's creatures, God's souls. How could any parent harm a baby? Or any grandparent for that matter?

The man's mother thinks of her grandchildren in the distant town, on the small island. They were not aborted. They are flesh of her flesh, blood of her blood. Illegitimate, born out of wedlock, against the laws of God and state, bastards one and all. Such names for her grandchildren, though they don't feel like her grandchildren. They don't have names, or faces, or ages, or even numbers. How many were there, anyway?

She doesn't know how to explain this to God, when they should meet, which will be quite soon, that she doesn't know how many grandchildren she has, or how they are doing. It will sound like a hell of a story. 'Excuse me, God, but the rules were . . .' The question, she explained after coming to a decision, was this: what is my duty to my God?

The man brought one of the children to his home village. The child was clean, literate, polite and delighted with her granny. The child did not look or feel or behave like the bastard of an adulterer.

Mind you, the priest was not invited to the meeting, and the neighbours, showing exquisite tact, did not come in, and the daughters were deployed around the area to keep the wife and children of the first family engaged. The first wife was marvellous about it. A mother could not deny her own son, she said. She hoped the matter would go no further than that. She too was entitled to her good name and standing. The first children were generous, adult, embarrassed and agonised. They did not want their mother hurt, or to quarrel with their granny or father, and they did not want to know the new arrival. Of course they had known about it for a long time. Teenagers are not stupid.

There was one thing on which everybody was agreed, except the man: they did not want to know the second woman. We have no polite terms in which to address her, no social skills with which to handle her, no formal position in which to slot her, no Church Apologetics to equal those of Mr. Debrett. We have no divorce, no remarriage and no room in which to breathe. Ireland is small, the towns smaller, the priests everywhere preaching the word of God and not a word from them about how to handle such a dilemma.

The opponents of divorce played the dilemma to the hilt. If everybody knew, and everybody did, someone whose marriage had broken down, we also know the financial consequences of it: breakdown impoverishes the wife and seventy-two per cent of Irish wives function as unpaid mothers in the home. The men don't earn enough to support two families.

The government offered women welfare in exchange for divorce. 'It's like asking turkeys to vote for Christmas', said Alice Glenn, a member of that government and a fierce opponent of the proposal.

The Catholic Church offered God's law: 'What God hath put together, let no man put asunder'. The government and pro-divorce campaigners started the campaign by agreeing with the statement. Garret FitzGerald proclaimed adherence to the Catholic faith and belief in life-long 'indissoluble monogamy', by which, we knew rightly, he meant marriage. He asked the people to distinguish between religious marriage, and civil remarriage in a registry office.

Jaysus.

This was akin to offering Christmas without Santa Claus. Everybody in Ireland knew that registry office weddings weren't the real thing. The few who embark on even a first marriage in that Godless office publish the banns in Gaelic in the newspapers, in the hope that nobody will be able to translate evidence of their intended pagan deed. We get married in churches. Even Protestants get married in churches. The Protestants joined in the campaign with an announcement that they wouldn't remarry divorced people before the altar.

In an effort to rally the turkeys, the government launched an offensive against farmers. If they divorced their wives, they'd have to divide the land with her, or pay a lump sum in compensation. The majority of Irish farmers tend a small acreage. Split it up and there'd scarcely be room for the hens. The women of course would keep the hens. The government's proposal did not please the farmers. They'd spent years waiting on their fathers to die, brother sitting brother out for it, and centuries waiting for the British to leave, while half the population starved for want of mere potatoes, and now the government wanted to divide the land still further. As for buying the wife out – Jesus Christ, it hasn't stopped raining this past two years, the hay is floating by the door even as we speak and we're dependent on EEC subsidies to keep going.

Besides which, at the end of the day, God says no, and there's an end to the matter. An *Irish Times* commentator, Howard Kinlay, writing after the vote confirmed Catholic laws for a Catholic people, showed how he hadn't been able to see the wood for the trees. He had cast his vote in the state-built, state-financed national Catholic school, which is named afer a saint. He then visited a friend in a state-built, state-financed, state-staffed Catholic hospital which is called after a vision of the mother of Jesus. His friend lay in a ward called after yet another saint. He then tuned into the state-built, state-financed and state-staffed radio station to hear how the poll was going and heard the twice-daily bells of the Angelus ring out, as a prelude to the news. Next day the results and analysis were interrupted on state-built, state-financed and state-staffed television to accommodate the playing

of the Angelus and a sixty-second long contemplation of a painting of the Holy Family. Catholics are more Catholic than the
bishops themselves, who live in palaces.

Doctor FitzGerald explained after the deluge why he had not
played the Orange card during the debate. It would have led to an
even greater defeat and confirmed the partition mentality. There
was a certain tragic truth in the observation.

It would have been like asking the second woman to Christmas
dinner. Imagine breaking up our own traditional way of life in
order to clasp to our bosom those who have brought the north
to the brink of civil war. Everybody knows that the Unionists are
bad people. Even the British don't want them. Unionists are, of
course, Protestants, but their religion is their own private business
and they mustn't be judged by their God. There is unanimous
agreement about this analysis. Lefties, liberals, politicians, priests
and even Protestants have reiterated it down through the years
and any contrary analysis – that the conflict in the north is
rooted in religious division – would be hurtful to co-religionists
of both faiths, and anathema to those of none. The northern
situation has nothing whatsoever to do with religion, so their
religious beliefs were left out of the referendum. Besides which,
the North doesn't approve of divorce. It was imposed on them,
after Stormont had been abolished, by order-in-council from the
mainland. The Rev. Ian Paisley agreed only last week, after the
referendum failed, that there were scriptural prohibitions against
divorce.

Well, he would, wouldn't he?

We have jokes about the implication of the anti-divorce vote for
the future of the Anglo-Irish agreement that seeks to bring north
and south together. First we bomb one million Protestants into
the Republic. Then we bomb one million Catholics out of it.

Laugh? Back at home, the granny nearly cried. She has reconcil-
ed herself with her God, her son, and the children of the second
union and she has kept faith with the only wife and she has not
hurt or insulted the second woman to her face. If she's lucky,
she'll die before that woman arrives on her doorstep. Let the next
generation handle that.

If only everybody could stay discreetly apart, observing the
borders, established by propriety, religion and pain, with blood
relatives meeting in private, hanging onto the notion of limbo,

and the assurance that God will surely look after us in death. To do other is to turn God's word in his mouth.

Some lefties think it would be better altogether to abolish God, especially the Catholic one. As well ask the English to abolish the Queen's title and role as Defender of the Protestant faith. Her son, too, had to settle for a private meeting, with no Mass, with the Pope.

—●—

Garret FitzGerald announced that he hopes to see divorce introduced before he dies. The man, now made redundant, rang his mother to say that he was emigrating to Australia. It is so very far away. His sisters will be unable to go see him if he should fall ill, or be lonely. His mother would like him to know, before she dies, that someone on the other side of the world will take care of him and love him. God forgive her, and God surely will, but she would like the consolation of knowing that he is in good hands. She will meet him, and his woman, on the shore, before the boat leaves.

—●—

Thirty-six point three per cent of the Irish people voted for the introduction of divorce. We are a young nation and a family and the growing pains are fierce.

New Statesman, 11 July 1986

Mary — Only a Woman

After Mary Murphy's husband broke her jaw and was sent to prison, she took her two children and left the family home. The state has told her that she is not a deserted wife.

Mary Murphy then had her marriage annulled by the Catholic Church. The state has told her she is still a married mother.

Mary Murphy subsequently had a child by another man. The state says she is not an unmarried mother, and that this child is legally her husband's child.

Mary Murphy says she doesn't care what the state calls her — prisoner's wife, deserted wife, separated wife, unmarried mother — the state can call her anything it wants providing it gives her an income of some kind for being a mother. The state refuses to do so.

She receives £40.35 per week as a discretionary payment, which the state can withdraw at any time. The minimum income for being a single mother of some kind is more than £50 per week. The Catholic church said, through a spokesman, that though she is, in the eyes of God, a mother, and not a wife, the church can do nothing for her.

Mary Murphy came to the *Irish Press* and asked for help. This is her story:

Born in Northern Ireland in 1951, herself the only child of a deserted wife, Mary left school at fifteen and trained as a hairdresser. At the age of twenty-three, she gave birth to a daughter. Unmarried and lonely, she answered a lonely hearts advertisement in *Ireland's Eye,* the family magazine which espouses traditional, conservative values.

She became pregnant by the man she wrote to within weeks of meeting him in Dublin in 1975. Six months after they first met, they married in church. She spent the honeymoon in the home of her surprised mother, who was not informed of the wedding, but was glad to see that her pregnant daughter had regularised her situation.

After the honeymoon, Mary and her husband went to live in his mother's home in Dublin. When the birth took place, Mary, her husband, their child, and the child of the first union, rented a private flat. Subsequently they were given a Corporation house.

Mary's husband, who was in regular employment in a city centre store, had started beating her after they left his mother's house. He began to drink heavily. She discovered that he had a history of mental instability.

Between 1975 and 1980 she was forced to obtain two court orders barring him from the family home. Promises of reform, family pressures, and desperation persuaded her on both occasions to have the barring order lifted, though their second child (her third) was stillborn when he kicked her in the stomach one week before birth was due.

In September 1980 her husband attacked her again. Her jaw was dislocated. All her upper teeth were kicked out. In October, he was sentenced to six months' imprisonment.

The state, which had deemed her in need of protection from her husband, paid her a prisoner's wife allowance while he was in jail. Her social worker states that she 'genuinely feared for her safety on Mr Murphy's release . . . he was a very intimidating and violent man who was unlikely to change. Mary saw no future in the relationship and feared for her own physical safety. I would earnestly support her case for Deserted Wives Allowance'.

She was so afraid that she abandoned the family home one week before her husband was due out of Mountjoy Jail. With the help and advice of her social worker, the two children were put into residential care in Madonna House, while Mary Murphy sought employment and a new place to live.

For two years, from 1981 to 1983, she supported herself by cleaning the homes of richer people. She earned enough to pay for a bedsitter for herself, but not enough to support two children, even had she been emotionally capable of mothering them. Because they were in care, she did not qualify anyway for the Deserted Wives Allowance. The law states that 'if she has no child dependent, she must be aged forty years or over'. Mary is in her early thirties. She visited her children regularly and sometimes brought them to her bedsitter for the weekend.

During 1983 she became pregnant by a man who refused responsibility for his child. He was, in any case, married. When she was too pregnant to work any more she applied for, and was granted, a single person's Unemployment Assistance, the lowest level applicable to people who have no stamps.

Her son was born in November, 1983. Her landlord did not want mother and child in the bedsitter. She put the infant in foster care for two weeks while she found other accommodation. After Christmas, she informed the state that she was not available for work, being the mother of a newborn infant.

She was struck off Unemployment Assistance and put on Supplementary Welfare Allowance, the discretionary payment that is available to people of no means whom the state is unable to classify. She had deserted her husband, said the state, and did not qualify for Deserted Wives Allowance. She was married, so did not qualify for the unmarried mother's allowance. She was unavailable for work, so fell through that net also.

At this point, she received a letter from the Catholic Church, informing her that her husband sought to have his marriage annulled and inviting her to present herself for interview to a church tribunal. In the event, her husband dropped the proceedings for annulment, but she decided to carry on with the interviews. She spent hours with priests, social workers and psychiatrists.

It was the considered opinion of the church, one not often delivered, and then only after exhaustive intimate inquiries, that her marriage had been defective from the start, and that it should be annulled. The judgement was handed down in August, 1985, and the annulment decree delivered to her in October of that year.

A church spokesman told *The Irish Press* that the majority of annulments are obtained by people who are poor. Although the number of annulments in any year hardly exceeds a dozen, the church spokesman was unable to say how mothers fared after their marriages were annulled.

There is no follow-up procedure to see how they manage financially. The church does tell the male partner of the annulled union that he has a moral responsibility to contribute to the upkeep of his now bastardised children, but, said the spokesman 'by the time the marriage is annulled, the husband and wife hardly speak to us, never mind to each other'.

In the case of Mary Murphy, in any event, it would be impossible to enjoin a moral obligation on the man whom she mistakenly married: the first child was not his, and both the first and second child are being cared for by the State. Why should he pay anything towards the upkeep of the third child, conceived of another man after his marriage was declared void?

As far as the state is concerned, of course, he is the father of all three children, because he is, in the absence of divorce, held to be the father of all Mary Murphy's children while she is married to him. She will be married to him forever.

On the other hand, says the state, he has not deserted her. It was she who left the home, though his presence in that home was so dangerous to Mary Murphy and her children that the state removed him from it and lodged him in Mountjoy.

Mary Murphy now lives in the upper floor of a Corporation tenement with the one child remaining in her care. She keeps the tenement scrupulously clean, as do the others living there. They have no bathrooms. A row of toilets on the second floor serves their bodily needs. The television reception in the house is lousy.

Mary Murphy contracted cysts on her bowel last Christmas. An operation proved unsuccessful. She attends hospital twice a week now to have them 'frozen' as she understands it, and the pain reduced. Her child attends a day nursery so that she can have some rest, on the instructions and advice of a local health nurse. Once a week she visits her other two children in Madonna House.

She observes all the outward functions of motherhood. She is not, says the state, a mother available for work, nor a mother qualified for assistance, nor a wife in need of assistance. In welfare terms, she is not a statutory mother at all. In practical terms she is not a wife.

She is, in the eyes of this country, a very poor person with no visible means of support, reliant on the charity distributed through the Supplementary Welfare Allowance. The recent Report of the Commission on Social Welfare recommends that all this fudging nonsense be swept away and a single payment be made across the board to all people without paid employment, with pro rata increases for dependent children.

The Report has been swept away, in turn. The Minister for Social Welfare has instigated an inquiry into welfare fraud. All the officials concerned with Mary Murphy agree that she is not defrauding anybody. Her problem is that officially she cannot be classified. Officially she's only a woman, and the wife of a brute, and that's her problem.

NOTE: Mary Murphy is a pseudonym.

Irish Press, 18 September 1986.

Mary was recognised as a deserted wife, and paid proper rates, as of 10 August, 1987. Her social welfare appeal was fought by Francis Barrett, barrister, acting on the instructions of family law solicitor Heather Celmalis. Both gave their services free of charge.

Dark silent nights

Mary Martin and her six children have been living without electricity in their Clondalkin, Dublin home since March.

The Electricity Supply Board disconnected them nine months ago because of unpaid bills totalling £307.15. Social agencies involved in her case indicate that her situation is near hopeless. She is, they say, at the very bottom of the poverty heap, and repeated attempts to rescue her have ended in failure.

The agencies are limited and hamstrung by welfare rules which prevent them giving Mary what she really needs. She needs money. She is as broke as it is possible to be in Ireland, in 1986.

When early winter darkness falls, her children go out into the street to play by lamplight. She sits in the benighted living room, by a small coal fire, the only flickering source of light or heat in an otherwise coal dark house.

She cannot read or watch television. She has no radio. From four o'clock in the afternoon until dawn next day, the woman sits in the silent heart of darkness. Those who visit her cannot see her face, unless she pokes the fire into flame, an expensive gesture, since coal costs money.

A neighbour, who brought *The Irish Press* to Mary's house, once saw the children burn their jumpers in the fire in an effort to provide heat and light. Often the children gather sticks on their way home from school, a difficult task in the urban streets of the capital city of the nation.

No candles have been allowed in the house since Mary's youngest child smuggled one up to bed and lit it in the middle of the night, in order to find his way to the toilet. The child left the candle burning on top of the foam mattress. Some of the children are too young to appreciate the dangers of fire, and too young to put on trust.

In a pitch black house, it is impossible to trace all the smuggled bits of candle that might be lying around.

In the depths of winter, it is safer to put the children out on the street, under the lamplight.

Mary Martin is in receipt of £79.55 a week from her departed husband, for herself and her six children. Were she classified as a deserted wife she would receive £126.85 a week. She does not meet that classification because the state has ruled that the marriage ended voluntarily.

It ended after her husband's final attack, which resulted in Mary receiving forty-nine stitches to wounds on her body. Rather than send him to jail, which would have meant an end to his job, and because the man had a heart ailment, the judge barred him permanently from returning to his family home.

In exchange the husband agreed to pay maintenance. That maintenance is of course well below the deserted wives' payment. The state is saving lots of money because a judge won't let the man return to beat up his wife. This man, says the state, has not deserted his wife.

Social workers say the problem could be solved if the government implemented the recommendations of the Commission on Social Welfare, which include a recommendation of one payment for all classes of dependents. That would allow Mary's maintenance payment to be topped up to the level other mothers are getting, who were lucky enough to be deserted.

In the meantime, Mary must sit in darkness for want of money. She has been disconnected several times in the seven years since a judge barred her husband from the house; a mishmash of payments via emergency allocations from the Health Board and contributions from St Vincent de Paul allowed the light to be switched back on occasionally.

Mary has also taken action herself. Like many in her area, she has learned how to reconnect the electricity in an amateur way. This is dangerous. She has often been caught. Last March, when the final disconnection came, Mary gave up. She approached no-one for help and sank into the dark.

Last Friday, in response to local agitation and a picket on its Ballyfermot office because of the numbers of families disconnected, the ESB announced that people's problems would be dealt with in a humane way if approaches were made to its various offices. One woman who did approach the ESB after being disconnected, and being caught resupplying herself, was asked to go to the ESB head office in Fleet Street.

'I was that terrified', she said 'I wet myself as I sat waiting to be called in'. The admission was relatively easy to make in the pitch-black of Mary's living room. No-one could see her face. Mary does not feel able to approach the ESB in daylight.

The ESB say that it cannot allow supplicants to be accompanied or represented by a companion when going to see officials. The ESB cannot see why people are afraid to approach them. This means that members of the Communist Party, who have collected petitions and organised pickets in Ballyfermot and Clondalkin cannot help the people who have come to them for help.

John Montgomery, a party member and a Corporation plumber, who says he literally smells poverty in his daily work, can only bring frightened women to his comrade Jean Roche, who tries in turn to put courage into the women. 'I am looking for a room in the area where women can meet and talk to each other and learn not to be ashamed of their condition.'

An ESB officer, one of the few in Ballyfermot who has met with widespread respect from both the Communist Party and the victims of poverty, has asked *The Irish Press* to ask the Communist Party to ask Mary if Mary will take the long walk, alone, to the ESB office. Mary says she is too poor to do it. She cannot offer what she has not got. She cannot afford electricity any more.

Social agencies agree that she is a good mother. Actually, she's a terrific mother, rearing six children by street lamp in Dublin, in 1986.

Derry City was burned down for less in 1968.

For reasons of confidentiality we have not used Mary's real name.

Irish Press, 4 December 1986.

Nancy O'Donnell

Athlone Urban District Council has instituted court proceedings to evict 19-year-old single mother from her council house. The case will be heard on October 16.

'It's a shame to see the sixth commandment broken in Catholic Ireland', says John Walsh, town clerk discussing the matter. 'I second that', says John Taaffe, county manager.

Their official reasons for wanting to evict Nancy O'Donnell are that she is a legal minor, and therefore unable to contract a tenancy agreement with the council, and that the family home she continued to occupy after her father died, is specifically designated for housing the elderly.

In fact, as the council admits, tenancy has been awarded in several cases to married couples under the age of 21, and a house designated for the elderly has already been awarded to a married couple, in their late thirties, with one child.

In fairness, too, the council has already allocated so many homes to single mothers that residents of the estate where they have been lodged, Battery Heights, have drawn up a petition requesting that no more single mothers be sent there.

Nancy O'Donnell does not live in Battery Heights, where the concentration of single mothers, deserted wives and families with social problems is such that few would live there, given the choice.

Nancy O'Donnell wasn't even given that choice, when the council took steps to evict her. They want her, simply, out of Marine View, a nicer class of residence altogether.

She got in there, after all, without serving the penitential time normally undergone by the desperate and the homeless damned. Tenancy of the house was given in March of this year to her father, Patrick O'Donnell, 55, a wheelchair-bound, very sick man, who had been on the waiting list for years.

While he waited, Mr O'Donnell had slept on the two seater sofa in the living room of his sister-in-law, Eileen Egan. The couch is less than three feet in length. He was unable to climb the stairs to one of the two bedrooms above, where he used to share a room with Eileen's only son.

In the other room used sleep Eileen Egan and Patrick's

daughter, Nancy.

The house is so narrow that each of its two storeys has only one front window.

Nancy and her father, and another daughter now married, had come over from Wales in 1974 to live with Eileen Egan when Nancy's mother walked out on the family.

'I was six and a half when it happened. My mother was supposed to take me into town on the bus that day. She didn't. She went alone and never came back. I don't remember her', Nancy recalls. 'My father was always sick after that'.

He was delighted when he finally got a house of his own, in Marine View. It had two bedrooms 'to suit his arrangements' John Taaffe admits. The arrangements were that Nancy would live with him and look after him.

She was known to be five months pregnant. 'My father just looked sad when my aunt told him', she says.

They moved in together in April. Mr O'Donnell paid one month's rent, spent one night there, collapsed, and died in hospital on Saturday, April 28.

Nine days later, the rent collector called, looking for the keys to the house. When Nancy explained that she was eighteen, he took two weeks rent from her, accepting that she was an adult. At that time the Dail was drafting a Bill reducing the age of legal consent from 21 to 18. It will become law soon.

On May 10, town clerk, John Walsh, told Nancy to get out. Her daughter, Leeanne, was born on August 8. Before the baby was four weeks old, Nancy had received a notice of eviction. 'It came just before my nineteenth birthday, on September 23'.

She is remarkably calm, for a teenage mother who has come through death, birth and proposed eviction in the space of five months. 'I studied in this house, alone, and sat my Leaving Certificate in July, though I had not been attending school since my father and I moved here'.

Given the other pressures, she was not surprised to fail all her subjects. 'I got six E's though. In different circumstances I might have done better'.

She is looking forward to her wedding next year to Peter Callanan, the acknowledged single nineteen-year-old father of her child. 'If we have any money, I want a three-quarter length beige wedding dress'.

Had Nancy's father lived for another ten years, Mr Walsh and Mr Taaffe admit, they might have taken another view of Nancy's tenancy, though they stress that succession rights are not automatic. 'It is at my discretion', says Mr Taaffe.

There is no need for stay-at-home daughters, the unpaid nursing backbone of this nation, to panic, they stress. Nor should under-age tenants in Athlone's council housing start biting their nails. 'We'll cross those hypothetical bridges when we come to them', says Mr Taaffe. One hypothesis at a time.

And if the council should win its case on October 16, what will happen to Nancy? Will they offer her alternative accommodation?

No, says Mr Taaffe.

However, he says, he has written to Nancy's aunt Eileen reminding her of her moral obligations to her kin. She is elderly, with high blood pressure, and has already reared two families, who have had their share of tragedy and ill health.

The council's moral obligations are etched in granite, on a plaque under a crucifix hung in the entrance to the Town Hall. Both were donated by the Ancient Order of Hibernians, in memory of one of their number, a 'public representative', who 'ever practised the precepts of Hibernianism, friendship and true Christian charity towards all'.

Irish Press, 4 October 1984.

Nancy and the man who can decide

There is a time to live and a time to die. It is not within the power of any human being to choose that time. 'God's will' we say here in Ireland.

There are some things we can control. The town clerk of Athlone District Council, Mr John Walsh, is in a position to exercise great control over the future life of Nancy O'Donnell, aged nineteen, and her baby daughter Leanne, aged eleven weeks.

He can have her evicted from her late father's council home, or he can give her tenancy of it. The local authority law on public housing allows him to act either way.

Nancy's father was given tenancy of a two-bedroom house in Marine View, Athlone, in April of this year. He and Nancy had been three years on the waiting list. By the time their new home was allocated, Nancy was four months pregnant.

They moved in. After living only one night in his new home, Mr O'Donnell collapsed, was taken to hospital, and died there a week later.

Local authority rules declare that a member of the tenant's family must have lived for two years in the council housed prior to the death of the named tenant in order to succeed to the tenancy. Clearly, in law, Nancy did not meet that qualification.

The rule, however, is not hard and fast. A town clerk can ignore it or enforce it. The reason for that rule is interesting. Sometimes, though rarely, a daughter or son living away from home hears that a sole surviving parent is on the verge of death, moves into the house and claims tenancy after the funeral. Authorities have to protect themselves against such unscrupulous behaviour, hence the rule.

Clearly, in the case of Nancy O'Donnell, the rule need not apply to her. The council knew for three years, while a house was sought for her sick, wheelchair-bound father, that she was meant to live with him. That is why he was given a two-bedroomed home – that she, like many a stay-at-home daughter, could live with him and care for him. The sacrifice of career and freedom that thousands of Irishwomen have made over the years, in order to live with and care for a sick parent, is well known. They are live-in unpaid nurses.

The National Plan assumes they will continue to do this. The Minister for Health, Barry Desmond, explaining that part of the plan, laid great stress on the number of hospital beds, and the millions of pounds, that will be saved if emphasis is placed on community care – moving patients back into their homes, where they would be looked after by the Nancy O'Donnells of this world.

Had it not been for 'God's will', Patrick O'Donnell would be alive today, housebound, and in the care of his daughter, to whom no doubt, Athlone Urban District Council would have been grateful.

Nancy is still alive, though, and so is her baby. She did not choose abortion. She escaped the fate of death by exposure, as happened in Granard. Her baby escaped death by exposure as might have happened in Kerry.

It is within the gift of John Walsh, the town clerk, to celebrate her decision to bring life into this world, to help care for her child, to reward her dedication to her father, and to alleviate her loss of the father who stood by her in her pregnancy, by giving her tenancy.

The law allows him to do this. The law allows him the merciful opportunity to emphasise that pregnancy outside marriage need not lead to bogholes and barnyards and police stations and courtrooms. It has been a bitter enough year for Irish women.

Athlone Urban District Council could ease the hurt of the blows that have rained down upon us by giving one mother and her child shelter from the storm.

Nancy faces eviction next Monday.

Irish Press, 25 October 1984.

We are blamed for something we did not do

Mary O'Rourke of Fianna Fail laid her political life on the line last Monday night in defence of Nancy O'Donnell, the single mother threatened with eviction. If ever a case had to be made for having women in politics, she made it, superbly.

The male councillors, who voted with her in a six to three verdict against county manager, Jack Taaffe's attempts to put Nancy out of her home, made an equally valid point – government by local representatives is necessary if we are to avoid government by remote control and bureaucracy.

'Life is short, only a few years, and you should not become entrenched,' Senator Sean Fallon of Fianna Fail gently counselled Mr Taaffe who had delivered a 20 minute lecture on rules and regulations, dating back to 1955.

The monthly meeting of Athlone Urban District Council provided a remarkable portrait of small-town Ireland. The nine councillors, intimately acquainted with each other and those who voted for them, had come together as a family might after a wake to discuss what should be done about the youngest, most vulnerable daughter.

The drama was cast in the shadow of Granard. Mr Taaffe was cast, and cast himself in the role of lawyer and bank manager who acted by the rules or acted not at all.

Mary O'Rourke, as chairwoman of the council, and head of the family had the most difficult part to play. It is the function of the chair, normally, to mediate between the council family and the manager, to smooth friction and reconcile. Somebody has to see that work gets done.

Last Monday night, Mary O'Rourke virtually abdicated the impartiality of the chair, and spoke as head of the human family.

'I do not agree with what you have done', she looked at Mr Taaffe directly, 'and you haven't done it in my name . . . you don't speak for me'.

She went on to speak as would any busy, anguished woman concerned with both affairs of state and affairs at home.

'I have been thinking and giving a lot of reflection to Nancy's case — I have lots of time driving alone between Dublin and Athlone — I think of Nancy tending her father . . . through the will of God, he died. If he hadn't, Nancy would be tending her father, and her own child, still tending both of them.

'I fail to see why a cruel stroke of fate should see her doubly penalised. She lost her father, she is threatened now with the loss of her home . . . natural justice puts her above the law. I ask you, manager — and I speak as chairwoman — to take the course that I know, I know so deeply, to be the correct course . . . let Nancy stay in her home'.

If Mary O'Rourke spoke as an older sister, the men rose as brothers. 'Nancy was the apple of her father's eye', said Sean Fallon, 'he would want her now to inherit his home . . . this case is unique, it will never happen again exactly as it has happened now — let the girl stay in the house, let her rear her baby in comfort and peace of mind . . . old Pat getting sick, the death — withdraw, manager from court at this late hour'.

Cllr Ciaran Temple of Fine Gael, rose to his feet. 'The young girl has had a child, God bless her, God bless her and her child . . . if her father had lived, the manager would have done nothing at all. And if he lived but another five years, would she not be left in peace then? I appeal to you not to go to court. Withdraw, manager, on human grounds'.

Cllr Ciaran Temple of Fianna Fail rose to say that he did not believe the manager would evict Nancy.

'His notice of eviction is in front of you', said Mary O'Rourke.

'I don't believe it', said Mr Temple.

'It's written in black and white in front of you, and it's being done in our name', said Mary O'Rourke.

'I don't believe it', said Mr Temple.

'I refer you to order No. 46', said Mary O'Rourke.

'When the manager sums up, I don't believe he will evict Nancy', said Mr Temple.

The manager summed up, insisted on eviction, and Mr Temple voted for him. Cllr Lennon, of Fine Gael , also voted for him, saying, 'she should have asked for help'.

John Keenahan, Labour, a large man in jumper, shirt and tie, spoke quietly. 'For the best part of three years I've been making representations for Nancy and her father against obstinate council management. They got the house . . . let Nancy be'.

Frank Waters, an independent, leathery, feisty, ex-postman, waved a letter. 'From the town clerk . . . telling me Nancy's house is designated for an old couple . . . I won't give their names. I'll say only that I have been fighting for this couple for sixteen years.

'I'm damned sure they won't take the house at the price of evicting Nancy, an unfortunate girl, with her child . . . this is low-down horse trading. Our city is being blamed for something we did not do, nor would we agree to. Over my dead body will Nancy and her baby be evicted. Call off this war, manager, against this young lady'.

The war will go on as Mr Taaffe made clear.

Athlone Urban District Councillors have made it clear that they stand as a family by Nancy. The Council for the Status of Women and Cherish sent telegrams in support of them and her. A Dublin family telegraphed Mary O'Rourke, 'Is there no room at the inn?'

The matter will come to court again on December 11.

Irish Press, 8 November 1984.

Nancy O'Donnell was given a council house in Battery Heights. She has since married the father of her child.

Purdah

They might as well have been in purdah. They gathered obediently for a mass photograph, revealing their faces but not their politics. The journalists who had come, by invitation, to look did not shame them further by asking questions. There was an unspoken agreement that it was the men who had brought them to this pass, and that it was the men who should be held accountable. These women had suffered enough.

They are the women who are stepping once more into the political arena, where a feminist can expect to be savaged this time round. The Women's Political Association invited them to come together publicly, to meet the press. The WPA offered to support them, regardless of party, in an effort to increase the number of women TDs in the twenty-fifth Dail. Those who accepted the invitation came to a reception in the headquarters of the Council for the Status of Women in Lower Mount Street last Thursday, 29 January, at 5 pm.

The timing was utterly and totally wrong. After seventeen years of involvement in the struggle for the liberation of women, during which women journalists figured prominently and brought a little expertise to bear, it still proved impossible for some feminists to pitch their demands properly to the media. The reception was given two hours after Charlie Haughey had revealed his election plans to the nation. The WPA was attempting to compete with that. Next day, the papers would be given almost exclusively over to what Charlie said, and the women candidates featured as an afterthought, an aside, a list of also-runners.

The reception had the air of a wake, without the relief of a corpse over whom we could lament and pour praise. No one wanted to probe too closely the bodies of the living dead. It will be hard enough for them when the landslide finally comes to bury them.

Or will it? Once in a while, in the course of that reception, we perked up. Monica Barnes, Nuala Fennell and Gemma Hussey were there, talking and smiling and fighting gamely on. Mary O'Rourke exuded confidence. Mary Harney was quite unafraid. Nora Owens bounced around. The newcomers were eager enough, and made themselves known to the journalists.

The talk, though, was searingly superficial. There were certain questions they did not want to be asked; questions the sympathetic media did not want to ask.

'I'd like you to meet a newcomer to our party' one elected representative, her seat under pressure, said to *In Dublin*.

If you do, we pointed out, we'll be obliged to ask her if she thinks that women are entitled to full pregnancy counselling, with information on all the options from adoption to abortion. We'd also have to put the same question to you.

It was a rotten moment. A man might have given a glib reply, shifted around, or even decried abortion as an option. This columnist has yet to meet a female politician, apart from Alice Glenn, who would deny absolutely the right to know. Why put the onus on the women to take full responsibility, though? Over the last five years it has been the women politicians who have taken the fiercest heat. So we agreed, the candidate and I, to keep silent counsel on the issue. We agreed not to talk. We accepted purdah.

Later another one would say to me 'Off the record, the first person to raise the issue of the closure of the clinics to me was a man. It was the first thing he said to me when I canvassed him. He was furious at the closure. Thanks for not asking me anything officially. It's been a bad five years'.

There was another matter no one wanted to raise. Outside the Council premises, on the doorstep, in the raw winter air, stood a group of young working-class women. The contrast between them, and the women candidates inside, was palpable. Their clothes were different, their accents were different, their addresses were different. They were the women of Sinn Fein, standing with Sinn Fein's only female candidate in this election, Pamela Kane from Ballymun, who is running in Dublin NorthEast. The WPA refuses to support Sinn Fein women, on the grounds that SF supports the use of force. Today the WPA refuses the right to know about Sinn Fein, said the leaflet these working class women handed out. Tomorrow will the WPA refuse the right to know about abortion? And the day after that, the right to know . . . about what?

Inside, it was agreed not to discuss the right to know. On the record. Or even off the record. Why force women candidates to admit that they're scared to speak publicly? Is it not the men who have brought us to this level, who have brought a situation where women carry the can for their malfeasance?

That reflection brought a sad reflection in train. Five years ago, before SPUC and the bishops and the men who bowed to them, women carried the can with panache, upending it at times over the craven political half of the species. Now on this day, Thursday 29 January 1987, women dare not speak about the right to know, and deny to others the right to speak. Between the politics of the womb and the politics of the border, we are caught between a rock and a hard place. No one in that room, that night, last Thursday, mentioned that the meeting took place on the eve of the fifteenth anniversary of Bloody Sunday, when British soldiers shot dead thirteen men who insisted on the right to know, and the right to speak. With such a terrible precedent, why would we? Life can be very hard, when you're reduced to the level of survival. This columnist lay on the floor, behind a closed Bogside door, protecting herself, when the shots rang out in Derry.

In Dublin, 5 February 1987.

Kerry Babies

The Kerry Babies Inquiry was set up to investigate how the police could charge Joanne Hayes with a crime she clearly did not commit, the murder of a baby found hundreds of miles from her home. The Inquiry shocked and surprised the public when it turned the bulk of its attention instead to the circumstances surrounding the death in childbirth, at home, of her own infant. 'Woman to Blame' by Nell McCafferty, gives the full story of Joanne Hayes and the Inquiry. These articles, written while it was in progress, show what she was going through at the time.

The Opinions of Mighty Medical Men

The Catholic Church will break its silence tonight on the Kerry Babies affair, when the parish priest of Kilflynn, who delivers the Sunday sermon at Abbeydorney, five miles down the road, will give an interview to the British television programme, *TV Eye*.

The investigative TV journalists have spent the last fortnight in Kerry examining the wider implication of the matter, with particular emphasis on sex education, contraception, and the situation of Irishwomen.

For the first time, the programme will show a headstone recently erected on the grave of the infant found on the shores of Cahirciveen. 'In loving memory of me. The Kerry Baby', reads the inscription. At the foot of the stone rests a plastic baby enclosed in a clear plastic bubble.

Tawdry though that image be, it is radiantly beautiful compared to the harsh realities of Dublin Castle, where the Tribunal of Inquiry hacks its weary bewildered way through the events of last year, the men sitting under an incongruously placed Bord Failte poster of Slea Head, off which the baby was allegedly thrown. Last week the public even got an inadvertent glimpse of a postmortem photograph of the Cahirciveen baby, held aloft by yet another expert on the length of umbilical cords and the weight of new born infants.

This man, using his hands held apart to indicate a certain length, as opposed to the length of the desk at which he sat, ventured a 'guesstimate' in centimetres, which was challenged by Martin Kennedy, counsel for the Garda superintendents, who had estimated the desk length in inches, whereupon Judge Kevin Lynch produced a steel tape measure, which the expert then used to satisfy their mathematical minds.

A second male expert, speculating on the angle at which umbilical cords might break or be cut, announced candidly: 'I haven't had the opportunity yet to pull a cord off a placenta'. Placentas are precious these days, you see, and are stored in deep freeze the minute they come out of the wombs, for use in heart surgery and such. The days are long gone when there were 'very well-fed cats in the Rotunda Hospital gardens because they used eat the placentas,' the first expert observed.

The atmosphere in Dublin Castle became quite clubby last week as first Professor Robert Harrison, professor of obstetrics at Trinity, and then Dr Declan Gilsenan, of the Midland Health Board, took the stand. Prof. Harrison even set a little test, inviting the men to work out for themselves the weight of the amniotic fluid in which a baby floated in the womb, given that its volume was '750-1,000' millilitres at birth.

Judge Lynch whipped his pocket calculator out. His mastery of detail, and ability to convert grammes into ounces, metres into yards, has been favourably noted.

The men had their moments of light relief during classes. After confessing that he found it quite distressing to look at the photographs of the dead Kerry babies, Prof. Harrison brightened up when Anthony Kennedy, counsel for the guards, asked him to examine a cutting from the *Daily Mirror,* which told the story of a woman who had twins by two different men.

'Which page?' grinned the professor. Page three pictures of naked women are a famous feature of British tabloids. 'Unfortunately,' guffawed Anthony Kennedy, 'there's no picture with it'.

How the other men giggled!

The men also discussed how a woman might look if she were carrying twins within her. Last January, in Tralee, when Judge Lynch asked a female nurse who had worked alongside Joanne Hayes in the Sports Complex if Ms Hayes had looked like she was carrying twins, Anthony Kennedy had objected technically to the idea of giving weight to the opinions of a 'mere nurse'.

Since then much time has been devoted to the opinions of mighty medical men, none of whom had ever seen Joanne Hayes pregnant.

Prof. Harrison disagreed with Tralee gynaecologist, Dr John Creedon's speculation that a woman bearing twins would necessarily have had 'a military bearing'. Some women were the 'mother earth types', who would 'strut and waddle', while 'others retain their femininity', said the professor who has very fixed ideas on what constitutes femininity.

As to paternity, the professor informed the legal men that wives aren't asked too many questions any more in the presence of husbands. 'We are well aware that the father may not be the father and one doesn't necessarily want to delve too much into that'.

One English hospital had found that 21 per cent of babies were not conceived by the men who presumed themselves to be the fathers. In the Rotunda, where he regularly delivers babies, Prof. Harrison often takes the precaution of not writing down answers given by women expecting twins when making arrangements for possible blood transfusions.

'You can never say somebody is the father. There are things nobody wants to talk about,' he told Martin Kennedy. Mr Kennedy didn't need to be told. The German expert whom he had dug up had never published his findings that 2.5 per cent of twins were conceived of different fathers. 'He said nobody wanted to know,' Mr Kennedy was woeful.

Anthony Kennedy had a message of consolation for deceived men everywhere. The German women who had twins by a German man and a black American soldier had been unable to claim maintenance from either 'as paternity could not be proved'.

Judge Lynch cut through the meandering about twins by different men by pointing out that Garda Liam Moloney had been unsuccessful in his attempt to halt the relationship between Joanne Hayes and Jeremiah Locke because she 'was so infatuated, or in love, that she would not entertain the idea of breaking it off'.

Garda Moloney's initiative had been undertaken in August, 1983, 'almost exactly at the time the third pregnancy was conceived'. Which, if the judge is correct in pinpointing conception, means that the Abbeydorney baby was born several weeks prematurely, thus clearing up the mystery of its light weight.

Weight, umbilical cords, fathers, lawyers and medical men apart, the judge then proceeded to what he thought was the heart of the matter. 'What sort of ladies are we dealing with here?' he asked Anthony Kennedy about the *Daily Mirror* women et al. 'We do not know', he answered himself. 'We do know here,' he referred to Joanne Hayes.

Joanne Hayes, who says her baby was born in a field, and Bridie Fuller, her aunt, who says the baby was born in the farmhouse, underwent psychiatric examination last weekend. Both women agree that there was only one baby born that night.

The psychiatrist's findings will be presented to the Tribunal which has spent eleven weeks now pondering the credibility of the Garda case that Joanne Hayes had twins by two different fathers, or the same father, one of which she secretly delivered herself in a field, the other of which her family helped deliver, stab and throw into the sea.

'You can never say somebody is the father', Prof. Harrison has told the lawyers and guards, all of whom are fathers. Will that affect their deliberations in any way? What sort of men are we dealing with here, after weeks of such information?

Irish Press, 28 March 1985.

Not Guilty Enough

The Kerry Babies Tribunal is nearly finished after seventeen weeks of intensive investigation of the mind, manners and morals of Joanne Hayes, without so much as a question asked about the minds and morals of the men who have perused, and pronounced upon, her since she was first brought to public notice.

Policemen, psychiatrists, doctors, and lawyers, all of them male, have been free with their comment on and speculations about this woman. Their own minds and assumptions have gone un-challenged. The men protected and respected each other right up to the end.

Though Joanne Hayes stands accused of no crime whatsoever, and was not on trial, her name has in the past months been bracketed with famed and anonymous figures of notoriety such as Myra Hindley, Malcolm MacArthur, a woman who believed that she had sexual intercourse with the devil, and in the closing minutes of the testimony of Superintendant John Courtney, with prostitutes.

Advancing his thesis that she was a woman of 'loose morals', about whom he could find no other man than Jeremiah Locke to testify, he said that in his experience 'the violent death of a girl with loose morals is one of the most difficult to investigate, because no man will come forward and say that they had an association with them. If there was a man who had an association with Joanne Hayes, it would be almost impossible to locate him'.

It was the sulphurous, unsavoury whiff of such testimony dur-ing the enquiry – will anyone ever forget the question posed by Martin Kennedy: 'Did she love Jeremiah Locke, or what he and other men were prepared to do with her?' – that persuaded the public to shower this woman with yellow roses, and mass cards, and hundreds of telegrams and letters, begging to be dissociated from the tone of proceedings that were being held in their name.

The most illuminating example of the male mind at work on Irish womanhood came perhaps from Dr Brian McCaffrey, Clinical Director of Psychiatry for the Eastern Health Board. 'She got herself pregnant on three occasions', he said.

She did not.

Joanne Hayes did not impregnate herself.

Nor was she artificially inseminated at the Well Woman Centre. (Please, Judge Lynch, don't prolong the Tribunal with another brain-storming session).

It merely slipped Dr McCaffrey's mind that men are responsible for pregnancy too.

He went on to say that Joanne Hayes was a 'princess-victim' figure 'the best example I have ever seen'. He had never actually examined her, or even exchanged the time of day with her, merely looked at her and read about her.

She didn't look right to him, given that she had admitted to the secret birth, death and burial of her child. 'It didn't have the impact on her that it would have on a normal individual'.

So now we have it.

Joanne Hayes would have cut a more impressive female figure entirely if, a year after her trauma, she were still sitting Siva. The doctor is not alone in his impressions. There have been mutterings that while in Dublin she went to the Dail, to a couple of pubs, and was even photographed smiling, on her birthday.

Dr. McCaffrey's colleague, Dr Fennelly, was quite explicit about this. He examined her in March and found that there was 'not a great degree of guilt at this stage, not as much as I might have thought she would have'.

She was possibly, said Anthony Kennedy, 'actually taking pleasure in her great struggle with the law and even taking pride in her accomplishment in winning, as she'd see it'.

Was she even, asked the judge, 'taking pleasure in the whole hubbub that we're all engaged in?'

Overall, nodded Dr Fennelly, the 'tribunal hasn't had a deleterious effect on her'.

'Which has to be abnormal in some way, to thrive on it', finished Mr Kennedy.

And this from men who have willingly posed before the television, even sitting specially after hours so that the camera could have a good long loving look at their egos on display.

This from men who burst out laughing when one of their number, a gynaecologist no less, regretted that the *Daily Mirror* cutting which was an official exhibit did not contain a page three picture of a naked woman.

This from men who pore over pictures of both dead babies of a morning session, and then repair cheerily to lunch to eat their fill and make witty conversation.

As why should they not? Gravity and grief about death can only be sustained for so long and then human nature will out, and we pick ourselves up and carry on normally. Those of us who have been through the harrowing months of this Tribunal have had nightmares and singing sessions alike.

Why was so very, very much more demanded of Joanne Hayes? Was it not enough that she cried her heart out in the witness box for a whole week, that she hyperventilated and vomited, and was sedated and was brought back for more, that she was imprisoned and lodged in a mental home?

Should she have refused the flowers, sent back the mass cards, spurned the letters that were sent her, rejected any morsel of comfort whatsoever?

What would these men consider 'normal' behaviour for a woman like her? The days when her name would have been read off the altar are long gone; women leaping onto the funeral pyre is not an acceptable custom here; in Iran, as one Irish judge remarked to a woman brought before him, females are stoned to death for certain actions which the men don't approve of.

We will never know now how exactly these men wanted and expected Joanne Hayes to comfort herself since she gave birth in Abbeydorney on the night of April 12-13, 1984. All we know is that she is not exhibiting a sufficient 'degree of guilt'.

Even though she stands accused of no crime whatsoever.

Irish Press, 16 May 1985.

Women and
Paid Work

Smoking can Damage
your Health

When the boss told them they couldn't smoke in the toilet any more, twenty women workers in Co. Kildare declared a strike, occupied the factory and joined a trade union. This morning, after a 12-day struggle that changed their world, they returned to work with a rise in pay, increased holidays and the strength of the ITGWU around them.

'We looked for three breaks, but two will do. There has to be give and take,' says Yvonne Moran. The union organiser for Kildare, Norman Croke, says: 'They're the best trade unionists I ever worked with; a joy to watch'.

Until Wednesday morning, 5 September, in the little Sport Tricot plant in Monasterevin, the women had been used to going to the toilet three times a day for an unofficial smoke and a chat. Apart from one tea break and lunch, they had been expected to sit in silence at their benches all day.

'We weren't allowed to talk, so the minutes in the toilet with a cigarette and a friend were welcome,' Martina Murphy explained. She had been doing it for eight years.

Then they were asked not to go in pairs any more. The women accepted this – you could be halfway through a cigarette and your pal would come in, so you'd light another to keep her company and the minutes would stretch.

On that Wednesday morning Martina Murphy went to the toilet area, not realising someone else was there, and the two were interrupted by Monica Kelleher, wife of plant owner Pascal Kelleher, who said that no one was to smoke there any more. A strike followed.

'It might seem like a small thing,' says Yvonne Moran, 'but you let yourself be walked over on a little matter like that, you'd be crushed altogether'.

There had been bigger issues over the years. In times of recession, if two members of a family were working at Sports Tricot, one was made redundant.

In a village with few opportunities that seemed fair – except, the women say, that the one let go was usually the one with most experience and higher wages.

The sequence of events, that Wednesday, as told by the women, followed the pattern of a family row. 'We stopped to talk about it', says Yvonne, 'and Pascal came round saying, "right lads, get back to work". We said we were on strike and he said we hadn't a leg to stand on because we weren't in a union. So we occupied the factory'.

They're not sure why. 'It's the kind of thing you see on television. There were those people in Woolworths', Martina says vaguely. Pascal switched off the power and went home.

The woman sat in the gathering gloom and gradually dozed off. Two of them, girls just out of school, had only been in Tricot for a fortnight. Their nerve failed and they burst into tears with hunger and cold. 'We told them to go on home, but it was very late and they were afraid of the dark so they stayed on'.

By dawn they were all sick from smoking. All day Thursday the occupation continued, though Pascal paid them their wages for the previous week.

He tore down a newspaper cutting that someone had brought in. The article told how a woman had appealed against unfair dismissal for smoking in England and been awarded £2,000 damages.

The father of one of the women contacted Norman Croke in Newbridge and he came down to the factory on Friday. After speaking to them he spoke to Pascal Kelleher and a meeting with the Federated Union of Employers was arranged. Norman then persuaded the women to leave the building.

He went with them to the FUE meeting, despite suspicion that they weren't really his members. A union doesn't recruit during a strike lest it be liable for strike pay. Neither Pascal Kelleher nor the FUE pushed the issue. They seemed relieved to be talking with a sensible man who at least got the women out of the factory.

Norman watched Martina 'look this FUE guy in the face and say "Do you have to ask permission to smoke? Are you forbidden to speak to your colleagues?" ' Unused to jargon, the women were devastating.

The men then made unofficial contact. A county councillor whom Pascal knew contracted a county councillor whom Norman knew and a settlement was negotiated before signatures were formally appended at a formal meeting with the women.

The agreed document is nearly forty pages long. It was a photocopy of one previously used by a multi-national company.

Mr Kelleher can say that smoking in the toilets thrice daily has been stamped out. The sweetener for the rule-bound women is a rise to union rates, four more days annual holiday plus two extra periods in the canteen, during which they can smoke their heads off if they want. They can well afford it now.

Irish Press, 27 September 1982.

Missus Mop

In four weeks' time, thanks to the politicians, teachers and pupils will get a day off, as their schools are transformed into polling stations.

The women and men who clean the schools will still be expected to put in a hard day's work. The men will receive more pay for this than the women.

Evita Brezina, of the Employment Equality Agency, has found that this amounts to discrimination and has recommended that the 154 women cleaners employed by the Dublin Vocational Education Committee should be given equal pay with the men, and that this should be backdated to 6 March 1982.

If Ms. Brezina's finding is upheld by the Labour Court, to which the VEC has appealed, the women will receive back-dated pay increases of £20 per week.

May O'Brien, women's affairs official of the Irish Transport and General Workers union, says the case has implications for more than the 154 women involved. All over the country, in other institutions, Missus Mop is being paid less than Mister Mop.

If a public service employer like the VEC is forced to deliver equal pay, the invidious distinction between 'women cleaners and male porters' will disappear.

Titles figured prominently in the case. The VEC argued that the women are 'cleaners/attendants' and that the men are 'general operatives'. The unions argued that the men are more usually described as 'labourers/cleaners' and that the title 'general operative' was dreamed up to justify the difference in pay.

Make a man a general and you conjure up visions of a war against dirt, where the males are in the front line, planning operations, taking grave risks, and performing above and beyond the call of duty. The women just come along behind, cleaning up the pieces.

Evita Brezina examined this proposition in the twenty-eight schools and colleges under the control of the VEC. In Colaiste Eoin, Finglas, she discovered that one woman (a cleaner) performed for a long period the same work as now performed by a male (a general). The only exception she found was that the woman did not climb ladders nor set up the gymnasium for examinations.

The VEC set great store by the feats of the generals going up ladders 'to take down light shades for cleaning' and change bulbs. Ms Brezina agreed with the unions that light bulbs don't blow all that often and examinations only take place yearly, which hardly justifies an extra twenty quid a week.

She added that whenever the gymnasium requires a special cleaning 'which is a very demanding job' the females rather than the generals are asked to do it, in addition to their other work.

The VEC argued that the generals have to cut grass in summer. Ms Brezina with admirable restraint did not ask 'what summer', but noted that many schools don't have grass to cut. While the men wait for the grass to grow, of course, all of the women are inside scrubbing, polishing and waxing floors.

The VEC pointed out that the generals are also expected to get onto a bus and travel into town to the VEC head office, carrying messages from school principals when necessary.

The unions noted stiffly that 'going on messages to Headquarters by bus is far more pleasant and easier than working in a tea-room or canteen', which the women are expected to do, while the generals troop into town on the 48A.

The VEC argued that the generals faced the very fires of hell in the cause of garbage removal because they were expected to 'burn such material in incinerators'. The unions replied that not only have women carried rubbish to incinerators, but 'some females . . . have in fact burned it'.

Ms Brezina cooled tempers by pointing out that 'only in some schools is rubbish disposed of in incinerators'. On the whole, people working in schools place rubbish in plastic bags like the rest of us, and there's and end to the matter.

The Equality Officer penetrated the very front line of operations, the School of Technology in Bolton Street, and the School of Trades, Linenhall Street, Dublin. There she found two generals working as full-time kitchen assistants. 'I am satisfied', she recorded in dispatches about the war on dirt, that the work done by the 154 women was equally demanding to that done by the two lads in the kitchen.

For all practical purposes within the meaning of the Employment Equality Act, helping in the kitchen was just the same as washing, cleaning, sweeping, polishing and tidying classrooms, offices, gymnasiums, libraries, halls, canteens, stairs, corridors, toilets, staff rooms, and cookery rooms, plus the furniture contained therein – desks, tables, chairs, floor covering, blackboards and cookers.

The generals did that cleaning work too, if they weren't full-time in the kitchen, the VEC pointed out, or catching the bus into town.

In conclusion, said the VEC, the generals are 'liable for transfer and are transferred'. Women are also theoretically liable for transfer, it admitted, but 'in practice this rarely if ever occurs'.

Ms Brezina examined the practice and the theory. She found that less than one male per year was transferred compulsorily by the VEC, and that many males voluntarily transferred from one school to another in order to work nearer home. 'Once they (the generals) reach the school of their choice, they remain stationed there . . .'

She could not find that men should be paid twenty pounds a week more than women for what turned out to be the privilege of living within walking distance of the job.

The VEC appeal against her decision will be heard in the Labour Court on February 2. The three unions involved, the Irish Municipal Employees' Trade Union, the Irish Transport and General Workers' Union and the Federated Workers' Union of Ireland, hope that their female members, the women cleaners in the dirt war, will be promoted to generals on that day.

Irish Press 22 January 1987.

The Labour Court upheld the women's claim.

Me Jane equal to you Tarzan . . .?

Irishmen have gone to great lengths to please and protect women, particularly the men from Cork who manufacture Kraft margarine.

It is cheaper than butter, they say, spreads more easily and enables women to make lighter than light pastry. Dowdall, O'Mahoney and Company Limited did not stop their efforts there. The subsidiary of Kraft Incorporated also offer us shortening cooking oil, fondant and bakery specialities.

The company men who guard the interests of women in the home are just as tenderly protective of the interests of women who work in their factory. No woman in their premises, packing away the margarine, is expected to lift an object that weighs more than sixteen kilograms.

The nimble work of wrapping a block of margarine is for females; the heavy work of taking away a case of margarine blocks is for men. There is a price to pay for such consideration, of course. Women in the home have to buy the margarine; the factory women who pack it are paid £30.80 per week less than the men who lift it.

Brian McGinn, an equality officer with the Labour Court, can do nothing about the price women pay for margarine. He decided in February, however, that the women who make it should be given equal pay with the men. He has awarded the nine female workers a £30.80 a week increase, backdated to 29 October, 1982, or from the day they commenced employment in the company, if it was after that date.

The Irish Transport and General Workers' Union is delighted with the decision. Equal pay cases on physical work comparisons are the hardest to win, and Mr McGinn has established a new set of criteria which should see Jane treated, at last, on a par with Tarzan.

It is expected that Dowdall O'Mahoney will appeal the decision, and try to bring us back to the jungle of strong men and nimble women, and two different rates of pay.

It was when wandering through that jungle, down in Cork, that Mr McGinn saw a sight that made up his mind. Tarzan had a job as Fondant Packer. He had a machine to help him. The machine took three minutes to fill a box with Fondant. Tarzan had to wait around during all that time, idly flexing his muscles, then he lifted the box and did what a man had to do.

Meantime, Jane was packing margarine busily into her box. She got no time to hang around at all, Mr McGinn noticed. Jane worked non-stop.

Furthermore, Tarzan's little box only weighed 12.5 kilos. The Factories Act 1955 sensibly recognises that a woman could lift that weight easily, and only forbade her from lifting boxes and such that weigh more than 16 kilos.

The company rallied to Tarzan's defence and pointed out that besides hanging around for minutes at a time waiting to lift a little Fondant box, Tarzan was expected at a moment's notice to swing across the factory and perform other tasks, such as 'stacking cases of margarine and fat, filling and manually transporting drums of oil, using a handtruck to move pallets of goods and materials about the factory bv ding, assembling orders for dispatch and some product preparation'.

This could fair make a man sweat.

Compare that, inferred the company, to the discreetly perspiring Jane, who just did non-stop 'light packing duties' with occasional breaks to clean, make canteen tea, collect and distribute laundry.

Mr McGinn found that in practice Tarzan stayed put at the task he was given the day he entered the jungle, 'largely because the individual men concerned prefer to remain on particular jobs and do not interchange'.

He pointed out that the company occasionally employed temporary Tarzans to do one task, and one task only, that of casestacking. The temporary Tarzans got paid just as much as the Fondant Tarzans or Fat Tarzans or Fondant cum Fat cum oil-drum Tarzans. The most standstill temporary Tarzan in the factory still got £30.80 a week more than the ever-busy permanent Jane.

'Yet any one of these individual jobs could require less effort than . . . the work performed by each of the women', snorted Mr McGinn.

Not only did the women and men perform like work, in terms of physical effort, but they both performed work of similar value, he signed off with a flourish.

Translated into English, the women are now saying 'Yipeeee' while the men go 'Aaagh-oh-agghh-oh-aaahh', and both sounds have been declared equal in value.

Irish Press, 26 March 1987.

The employers appealed the decision to the Labour Court, which has not yet ruled on the matter.

Three Months Later

For three months now, through summer heat and autumn rain, ten women workers and one man have been on strike against the Henry Street store of Ben Dunne.

They obeyed a union direction not to handle South African fruit. One of them was suspended, and the ten others came out in sympathy with her. None of the workers in Mr Dunne's other forty six stores followed the union direction; nor has the union asked them to strike in support of their colleagues.

'There's no point my calling them out, because they wouldn't come,' says Irish Distribuitive and Administrative Trade Union boss John Mitchell. The question arises, in face of the martyrdom of his eleven young followers, why the union asked workers to do something which the union knew the vast majority of them wouldn't do.

'That's a good question,' says Mr. Mitchell.

He didn't give an answer.

The strike has less to do with a principled trade union stand against apartheid and its attendant evils, than with the efforts of the IDATU to revive its ailing fortunes.

Before John Mitchell came from the ESB Officers' Association to take over the £29,000 a year job of running IDATU, the union had been losing members hand over fist. It was conservative, complacent, and a lap dog of management. Members transferred to unions willing to fight for their rights.

Mr Mitchell, a fiery and combative radical, was brought in eighteen months ago to stop the haemorrhage. He did.

This year, at the annual conference of IDATU, the union decided that its members should not handle South African produce as a protest against apartheid under Mr Botha. The decision was taken by a handful of the thousands who comprise the membership of IDATU. That, of course, is perfectly normal and democratic. Everybody can't go to conference, so the few speak on behalf of the many.

The few in this case – as in all conferences – were made up of politically committed delegates and the union leadership. That too, is normal, but it leads to problems, such as committing the rank and file to things the rank and file hasn't thought about.

The current problem for Mr Mitchell is that a decision was taken at the top level and handed down and the lower ranks want nothing to do with it.

He is left with eleven workers on strike against nearly impossible odds, while their hundreds of colleagues work steadily on.

Looked at another way, of course, it's no problem at all. The IDATU is getting massive publicity and a reputation for militancy at the cheap cost of £21 per week strike pay per worker. Three months media coverage and more to come for an outlay of £231 a week on eleven young people is a bargain.

Those who did heed Mr Mitchell's call have been left to carry a lonely burden. Their bodies bear the bloody bruises of confrontation with scab labour, management, and the guards, as they try to stop goods being brought into the store. Far from being discouraged they dress now in newly bought oilskins and wellies, in preparation for a long, cold, wet winter on the footpath.

'Between strike pay and what they get from collections, they're nearly as well off as if they were inside working,' says John Mitchell. He says this about workers who used take home £91 per week, who subsist now on £21 each, plus what they divvy out from the little they collect from sympathisers.

They deserve more support from a union which is profiting so massively in their name.

Irish Press, 11 October 1984

Three Years Later

Last Saturday the Dunnes Stores strikers, ten women and one man, started their third year on the picket line. During the twenty-four months that they've been on protest against the sale of South African fruit by Mr Ben Dunne, their stand has caught the imagination of the whole world. From Durban to Delhi to Derry, people have asked why they went on strike and gone on from there to ask why apartheid exists, and what can be done to stop it.

The fact that the strikers were mostly female has further fired curiosity. It is an extraordinary thing to see young females, who were teenagers when the strike began, keep up the fight through hail, rain and shine. People expect teenage females to have other things on their minds, like boys and clothes and sex and the diamond ring that will lead to marriage.

The eleven strikers changed these expectations. They have upheld not just the dignity of black people, but the dignity of half of the human race who have long been dismissed as frivolous.

In that context, the recent remarks of a White House politician show how shallow the male mind can be. Donald Regan, no relation to the President, but obviously a close mental cousin to judge by what he said, explained to reporters that sanctions against South Africa would fail because women couldn't be relied upon.

Women, he said, would never give up their diamond rings. Women have diamond rings on their brains, you see. A diamond ring means marriage and status. South Africa is the world's largest manufacturer of diamonds. If we were to impose sanctions, there'd be no more diamonds, therefore no more diamond rings, and women just wouldn't stand for that, particularly not Yankee women.

'Are the women of America prepared to give up all their jewellery?' asked Mr Donald Regan.

No, he answered himself. Blacks must therefore suffer.

The men can't help them, because the women would object.

There was a time when remarks such as those made by Mr Regan could be dismissed as nonsense, and the aberrations of one silly male. When one links them to remarks made by other men, in other countries, however, one can see that these guys sincerely and truly believe what they say.

Everything, everywhere is the fault of women.

Adam, say the men in frocks, was brought down by Eve. She just wouldn't give up apples, and she made him eat one too. The Coalition of 1982, says Garret FitzGerald, was brought down by Irishwomen. They just wouldn't give up wearing children's shoes, and avoided paying tax on adult footwear. The most dangerous place in the world was a mother's womb, said Bishop Joseph Cassidy, inveighing against abortion – men have nothing to do with pregnancy.

Mr Regan's thinking is all of a piece with such logic. It infers that as soon as the Dunnes Stores strikers come of marriageable age, they'll forget about oranges and start thinking about diamonds, and will abandon the picket line before you can say 'I do'.

They'll just grab the first men they see, and force those poor guys to walk into a jewellery store and make them buy rings. The blacks who mine the diamonds for those rings can go hang then, as far as women are concerned.

It does make sense, doesn't it? Look around you and see who's wearing diamonds in your street, or village, or town. At the nearest farm, where the animals are starving for want of fodder, and farmers are on their knees, and the eyes will be taken out of your head by the flash from the finger of the farm wife.

You don't see any men wearing diamonds, do you?

You don't see any men having abortions, do you?

You don't see men wearing children's shoes, do you?

And if they are eating South African apples, it's because the women did the shopping. Since the beginning of time, it's the women who went for the apples, and it's women now who are insisting on diamonds, and as soon as the Dunnes Stores strikers grow up, they'll be just like the rest of them. One more year on the picket line, and you'll see. Wouldn't be surprised if they run off to Birmingham with a black man, skin as black as coal, as the song says. Black men after all, are the only ones who seem to praise the women these days. 'They've provided a beacon of hope to us in South Africa', said Bishop Desmond Tutu in a message to the strikers. He would, wouldn't he? He's black, he lives out

there, and he wants the whites of the world to impose sanctions.
He doesn't understand why we can't. It's because diamonds are a
girl's best friend. Simple, as the Americans would say.

Kerry's Eye, 18-24 July 1986.

*On 1 January 1987, the Irish Government banned the importation of
all South African fruit. The strike was brought to a successful conclusion
on that date.*

Glen Abbey gets Knotted

When Glen Abbey put a woman in tights, in a cage, in a television advertisement some time ago, such a storm of protest was unleashed that the company quickly released the video star and be-stockinged women were henceforth accepted as free females exercising 'Rogha na mban'. Women's choice hit the bill boards. The Rape Crisis Centre was well pleased.

Anne O'Donnell, publicity officer, was one of three members of the Centre whom Glen Abbey invited along to their boardroom to discuss the company's future advertising campaigns.

She has not had such a good time, she says, since the days when she was a rank and file protestor of Irishwomen United, the radical feminist organisation which occupied the offices of the Federated Union of Employers in the mid-seventies to demand everything and achieve nothing, except the satisfaction of watching men in pinstripes ask themselves in frustration just what it is women want?

Now, in the board room of Glen Abbey in the 80s she heard the men admit that their ignorance of feminist feeling had cost them a fortune. The production and subsequent withdrawal of the Glen Abbey caged woman video had led to a loss which the company estimated conservatively to be in the region of £15,000 to £18,000.

When the video was first shown on RTE the station was deluged with dozens of phone calls from individuals. It was the Rape Crisis Centre and CASE (the Campaign Against Sex Exploitation) which went about lobbying in an organised way, writing a formal letter, detailing their objections to RTE, to the Advertising Standards Authority in Kildare Street, Dublin, and to the advertising manager of Glen Abbey.

After the offending advertisement had been withdrawn, Glen Abbey wrote to the Rape Crisis Centre offering formal thanks for having taken the trouble to send a signed letter complete with chapter and verse. The company invited Ms O'Donnell and two of her colleagues to come along and discuss advertising with them.

The three women enjoyed a rare ninety minutes of feminist bliss in the company of a Glen Abbey management representative and three representatives of the advertising company which dreamt up the video.

'The man who actually conceived of a woman in a cage, wearing tights, wasn't there', she recalls. 'He had been literally rendered sick by the opposition which sprang up in protest against the fantasy'.

Ms O'Donnell and her companions went meticulously through Glen Abbey advertisements past present and to come, pointing out what was good, bad, indifferent, effective and merely shallow. 'We even got into the area of quality of tights. If you want to know which Glen Abbey tights are good value, ask me. I'm expert now' she says.

For its part, Glen Abbey darkly remarks that the video campaign was withdrawn after pressure from RTE, not the women, and points out sourly that Glen Abbey has not since advertised on the station.

Once bitten 13 months shy, is the moral suggested.

The 'copy committee' of RTE, whose job it is to vet advertisements for general acceptability, acknowledges that it requested Glen Abbey to witness the video after a substantial volume of complaints from viewers. The obvious question arising from that is, how did the copy committee let the video through in the first place?

Peadar Pierce, chairman of the four-man committee, says the committee learns from its mistakes all the time. This, he protests, albeit weakly, has nothing to do with the fact that the committee is exclusively male.

He feels, his voice fading away as he speaks, that men are as capable of spotting sexism as are women – except once in a while. It was on foot of formal protests from the Rape Crisis Centre, he then confirms,that a radio advertisement for National Aluminium Windows was to be withdrawn.

The advertisement featured a voice-over from Gloria Hunniford extolling the virtues of iron framed windows. 'They'll never get at her now' a male voice said as she faded away.

The Rape Crisis Centre pointed out that the suggestion was rapacious, inviting speculation that women were objects to be raped unless they spent money protecting themselves. The male voice at the end of the advertisement was subsequently dropped, though the company protested, and Mr. Pierce wonders still if perhaps the company was right, that it merely meant to suggest that celebrities needed protection from the public, not that women needed protection from rape.

Men are not aware of the subliminal desires, Ms O'Donnell suggests crisply. The Rape Crisis Centre offered a feminist volunteer to help the RTE all-male committee with their deliberations twice a week when the new advertisements come in.

Mr Pierce, assistant sales controller of RTE, says this is not acceptable, since the station must remain free of outside control, a valid point.

His explanation of the absence of RTE women on his committee is much less valid. Members must be drawn from management structure, he says. 'There are no women at management level in the advertising sales department of RTE', he confirms in the next breath.

He cannot see his way to involve, in a permanent capacity, non-management women while RTE struggles monolithically and chauvinistically towards equality of employment of women in the station. So once in a while when he suspects an advertisement of being sexually offensive, he invites female employees to give their opinion.

The trouble with that approach, obviously, is that the four-man committee occasionally lets through advertisements which, as men, they consider perfectly acceptable. Advertisements such as that dreamed up by Glen Abbey and National Aluminium, the subsequent withdrawal of which cost a fortune all round to the men who conceived them, and the man who then aborted them.

Until the men come to their senses, and involve women at all levels, the Rape Crisis Centre will monitor their fantasies and protest at their excesses. Women, says Anne O'Donnell, have power at their fingertips. All you have to do is organise, agitate and protect. Acting together, women's groups could change the public face of females in this country.

Irish Press 21 March 1985.

Two women have since been appointed to the RTE five-person copy committee.

Death to the Union

The little roly-poly woman in Buswell's Hotel was telling a trade union tale that was much like other trade union tales. How she helped organise the first factory she worked in, where they made sweets; the struggles they were now engaged in at the bakery where she worked on the biscuit line.

For the past eight months she has been telling her story to whoever will listen. It is not easy to get an audience because she speaks only Spanish, but interpreters have always turned up to help. So far, she has told her story in Norway, Sweden, Denmark, France, Spain, Greece, Portugal, Holland, Italy, Switzerland, and this week she is in Ireland.

The English turned her away at the port of entry, saying that she was just another foreigner looking for a job. In Germany she got lost, having taken the wrong train, but she showed phone numbers to people and was afforded help by kind strangers.

She drank iced water in Buswells, refusing tea, coffee or alcohol, and she did not smoke. Iced water with a slice of lemon is a treat where she comes from, she said. Wherever she goes, she distributes the newspaper of her trade union. It is called 'Boletin' and it is printed in Spanish. They can't afford foreign language editions.

She didn't notice the other people sitting around the lounge, did not take the time to cast lingering curious glances, the way one might when travelling the countries of the world. Her world envelops her urgently wherever she goes. All she wants to do is tell whoever will listen about her trade union in El Salvador.

Her colleagues back home hope that when she returns in the autumn she will bring with her tidings of how people in all the countries she has visited are demanding the release of nine members of her trade union executive, who were sentenced to indefinite detention by a military tribunal.

Originally, 115 of them were arrested, as they attended a trade union congress on 19 January, of this year, but these nine are the ones who remain in captivity.

The little woman's task is daunting, speaking only her own native language as she does, and carrying newspapers that the rest of us can't read, but she points to the photographs to show that the workers of El Salvador are organising, just like other workers in the world, and she picks out of one photo crowded with banners the banner of her own union. The words read 'Federacion Sindical Revolutionara', which means Revolutionary Trade Union Federation.

She was a little hesitant about the translated sound of her words. 'Revolution, socialism', the interpreter was saying in Buswells, which is just a stone's throw from the Dail, where on that very day the Minister for Foreign Affairs, Mr Barry, had formally apologised to Mr Reagan about someone burning the American flag, and added in the same breath that things were better in El Salvador since the recent elections there.

This woman didn't know Mr Barry had said that. She doesn't know who Mr Barry is. But she knows, as a result of her travels, that El Salvador is frequently linked with communism, Cuba and the USSR. So, she is hesitant about using words like 'socialism' and 'revolutionary' when she describes her struggle to get better wages for making sweets, or an eight-hour day while making biscuits, although they are terms she frequently uses.

Sometimes her union demands more than improved working conditions. After the coup in October 1979, for example, the workers occupied her sweet factory demanding a return to civilian government, the army came to her factory and took her and two others away to police headquarters. For three days, at 15 minute intervals, electric shocks were applied to her breasts and her anus. They made her watch the others being similarly treated. Then one night, they brought her out into the yard and made her sit on an ant-hill. Afterwards, she was put into a cell filled with excrement. Then she was released.

Five days after that her 13-year-old daughter was shot dead while standing at a bus stop. The woman left home, so as not to attract further attention to her family; her husband also left home, her mother looks after the two remaining daughters. The woman also left the sweet factory, and picked coffee beans out in the country for a while. The work nearly killed her, she grinned, as she was not cut out for agricultural labour.

So she went back to San Salvador, pleased to be in the city and began to make biscuits. The army doesn't kill everybody, although 50,000 have died between 1979 and 1984, and a person can survive the way people do survive in every country where bullets fly.

There was a whole lot more she could have said about the political situation in her country, she explained, but basically her job is to gather support for her nine imprisoned comrades, and for her union's right to organise and engage in strikes and such like.

Come September, if nobody notices or objects, she'll get back to making biscuits. She's very ordinary, very small, she moves from trade union to trade union around Europe, giving out her Spanish 'Boletin' not understanding a word anybody says to her.

She is thirty-two years of age. Her name is Christina Marin. She'd break your heart, she is so ordinary.

Irish Press, 4 July 1984.

Death to the Women

On this, the eve of the New Year, the most precious thing we can wish each other for 1987 is good health. With AIDS spreading as it is, we'll have to keep more than our fingers crossed. Good wishes will not be enough. A woman who ought to know is May O'Brien, Equality Officer for the Irish Transport and General Workers Union. She sits on one of the top floors of Liberty Hall in Dublin, a location commensurate with her high standing among the powers that be in the land. In her long career she has met with bosses and union leaders who command respect in the community – the kind who are known as pillars of society.

When she speaks of such men, therefore, we can be sure that she knows what she's talking about, and of whom. In the dying months of 1986, as the deadly threat of AIDS among us was officially acknowledged, she spoke out about it. She is a modest, mature, respectable woman of senior years. This is what she said:

'We talk about AIDS requiring "responsibility" so the need arises for constancy or faithfulness between couples. That, over many years, is what women gave, while their menfolk had their flings at the business conference or the union conference. Women now worry about AIDS knowing from old how irresponsible their menfolk may be when it comes to sex.'

There is the nub of the matter – how many men can put their hands on their hearts and swear that they have known no woman but the marriage partner? How many will admit that they have known another? How many will submit themselves for AIDS screening to ensure that they do not carry the killer virus, picked up, possibly, on some foreign junket?

Not many.

Despite that, the Catholic bishops, here and in England and in America, say that the use of condoms is sinful, though it be the only protection available against an infected man. They ask us to trust the men, and take their word that they have been faithful down the years.

You might as well ask turkeys to trust in Christmas.

The fact is that any Irishman who has been unfaithful to his wife in the last five years is a potential carrier. He does not know, after all, who he's been with, in the sense that he does not know the other woman's history (or the other man's – many a husband has engaged in homosexual intercourse).

It is all very well for the bishops to shout against condoms, but at this stage they are asking a woman to risk more than her own life. They are asking her to risk the life of her unborn child. Isn't that a grand turn-up for the books? In 1983 they asked us to oppose abortion, so as to save the life of the unborn. Now they're asking us to oppose condoms, though doing so might kill the unborn.

Plus the mother.

Mother and child must risk death so as to preserve the figment that Ireland is a land of saints, scholars and faithful men.

AIDS, by the way, can lead to a very smelly death. The body's system collapses and leaves it open to all sorts of ravages. The kind that slayed Henry the Eighth. Should we risk that for want of a hygienic piece of rubber?

Will the bishops approach our coffins?

Kerry's Eye, 25 December-1 Janyuary 1987.

Cory Acquino

Much will be asked of Cory Aquino, the new President of the Philippines. Much has already been made of those in need – the peasants with no land, the scavengers on the rubbish dumps. Even President Reagan will get a hearing, looking to have his American bases kept open beyond 1991.

The litmus test of her rule should be what she will do for those with no claim to land, not even a place on the rubbish dumps – the women who have been reduced to selling their very flesh. There are tens upon tens of thousands of Filipino women who have had no option since puberty but that of working as prostitutes. Daughters have worked alongside their mothers and grandmothers at this dreadful job since Marcos made the Yanks welcome to the islands. Alongside the American military bases, whole towns have grown up that are peopled almost exclusively by females, and it is the open function of those females to service the perversions of soldiers and tourists. So urgent has been the need of the women who work as prostitutes to do something, anything, to feed themselves and their children and their children's children – for the birth rate among young girls is horrendous – and so destitute their lives, and so futile their prospects of ever having any other job, however menial, however subsistent, even the subsistence of the leavings of a garbage pile, that the Roman Catholic church itself regards them with a benign eye.

Even the priests, familiar with the poverty to which the people of the Philippines have been reduced, have recognised the desperation of the situation which drove women to sell themselves.

Much has been made here in Ireland, in recent years, of the desperation which drove Irishmen to use their flesh in defence of their right to live. The hungerstrikers had nothing left but their bodies, and they used their bodies, allowed their flesh to be consumed, and diseased, and wither away.

They were regarded, rightly, as heroes.

They befouled themselves, that life might go on, if not for them, then for others.

There is a sense in which the prostitutes of the Philippines are heroines. They befouled themselves, and were befouled, that they might hold onto life; their own lives and those of their dependents, the thousands of men, women, and children who were related to them, as husbands, fathers, brothers, grand-fathers, sons, sisters, daughters and relatives to the second remove, for the Philippine social system is rooted in the extended family.

Over the years the prostitutes have become diseased, calloused, and weakened; they have been beaten and they have died. Their bodies have been used as the receptacles of sexual organs and perverted artefacts, the repositories of drugs and unceasing flows of semen, as men by the dirty dozen used them daily for the 'rest and recreation' so beloved of American soldiers and businessmen abroad.

It is difficult for citizens of the West to conceive of the scale of prostitution in the Philippines, and the depths of poverty which drove women to engage in it. It is even more difficult, culturally, to appreciate the enormously casual attitude of 'our boys' to the damage they wrought over there, our boys being a term that ap-plies as much to the plane loads of Irishmen who talk about a Bangkok holiday (bang-cock, geddit?) as to President Reagan's lads.

It is something that will not be much talked about in months to come, as the West monitors the arrival of democracy after Marcos, for democracy there, as here, will be measured in what is done for the man – the peasants, the farmers, the workers, the guerrilla fighters who return home.

The true test of Cory Aquino should be what she does for the prostitutes, the women who, having nothing else, had to sell their very flesh in order to live.

In Dublin, 6, March 1986.

We have been brought to
our knees

The month of February was a lousy one for the working class. It was so bad, blow landing upon them after blow, that the devastation has gone unnoticed, because it was so widespread and numbing.

It began in England, outside Fortress Wapping, where the *Sunday Times, The Sun* and other newspapers in the Murdoch group are printed. The printers who were sacked by Mister Murdoch, and replaced by machines, had been picketing Fortress Wapping for over a year. That strike ended last month, with total and utter defeat for the printers and their union. The ending of the strike meant the ending of a great and glorious era of the working classes, which began in Germany in the last century, and spread throughout the world. The Trade Union Movement began in Germany. It was founded on a simple precept – the working class have only their labour to sell, and the labourer is worthy of hire.

Mr Murdoch, with the help of Margaret Thatcher's anti-trade union laws, put an end to such uppity working-class notions. The skilled labourers were brought to their knees and smashed.

The domino effect of one trade union falling and others being knocked down in turn was felt here in Ireland. Last month the workers of Packard Electric were also brought to heel. They went on strike and were given a massively simple and humiliating choice – give up the strike or give up your jobs. Their multinational boss threatened to close down the factory. Why not? There are other workers, in other countries, so desperate for a job, any job, at any price, that the multinationals can relocate before you or I could say 'The labourer is worthy of hire'.

The Packard workers, acting on the advice of their broken union, gave up the strike and went back to work. They were not allowed onto the factory floor until they had each signed a promise that they would not go on strike for another two years. The word of the union, and the word of the worker, isn't even good enough any more. The boss exacted their signatures on the dotted line.

The month ended with working class people around this country, and England, and the countries of all of Europe, literally joining the bread-lines. They were queueing for the free food which the EEC is now doling out to alleviate poverty. Photographs of the working class on the bread-line were printed in all the European newspapers without so much as a hint at the horror of it, or an acknowledgement at the shame of it.

We have not yet recognised what has become of us. We have not understood that we have been brought to our knees. Adults with only their labour to sell are not allowed sell even that, and have been forced to stand in line, in the open, for a portion of meat and cheese and butter.

Meantime, Ronald Reagan sells arms to Iran and the Iranians use the surplus arms to blow up Americans in Beirut, and Ronald Reagan uses the profits from the sale to blow up Nicaraguans, who have done the one thing he hates − the Nicaraguans have formed a government devoted to the working class.

To whom shall our government be devoted when and if a government is formed next week? Beware the Ides of March.

Kerry's Eye, 26 February 1987.

A minority Fianna Fail government was returned.

North

The Peace People at War

On the day that Anne Maguire cut her own throat with an electric carving knife, 18 January 1980, her sister Mairead Corrigan was in her flat on the Cavehill Road, preparing for a three day trip to Cambodia, where she hoped to join Joan Baez and others in a symbolic march, bringing food supplies to refugees. A priest telephoned her around four in the afternoon to tell her of Anne's death. She went to the Maguire household.

Betty Williams was in a neighbour's house in Finaghy, bringing a present to a young woman who had just given birth to a baby girl. Peter McLachlan telephoned her there and she returned home to 'open a bottle of gin and sit up all night' with a New Zealand woman who had flown over to join the Peace People one year before, had since resigned, and was now working as paid housekeeper in the William's household.

Ciaran McKeown was painting the windows of his home, which had that morning been declared suitable by the medical authorities for the imminent home birth of his seventh child. He received a telephone call from Peter McLachlan, then in the Peace headquarters, and he went that evening to the Maguire household where he met Mairead and Peter.

Kathleen Lennon, whose son Danny had been shot dead by the British Army while he was driving the car that subsequently smashed into Anne Maguire and three of her children in August 1976, had just returned from Long Kesh, where she visited one of her three remaining sons, all of whom are now in custody, on long sentences, two of them on the blanket. She heard the news on television. She then went out to work on a part-time night cleaning job, leaving her husband at home.

Within a month of Anne Maguire's suicide, Betty Williams resigned from the Peace People. Peter McLachlan was voted out of it. Mairead Corrigan was voted Chairwoman of what remained of the movement, and Ciaran McKeown was preparing to withdraw from all leadership functions to write a book on world peace. Kathleen Lennon continued to visit Long Kesh and attend rallies organised by Provisional Sinn Fein against H Block.

Peter McLachlan was out of work, his reputation as a business person suffering from the Peace People's declared lack of confidence in him.

Betty Williams was also out of work, separated from her husband, her personal finance in a troubled state. She hoped to support herself and her household by monies earned from future lecture tours as a Nobel Peace Prize winner. Ciaran McKeown had reached voluntary redundancy on the Peace payroll and was earning his living as a freelance journalist. Mairead Corrigan, now living in the Maguire household and helping to look after her dead sister's three remaining children, expected that she could exist simply for the next three years on that money which remained to her from her £38,000 share of the 1977 Nobel prize money. Kathleen Lennon was receiving visits from social workers about the contentious matter of rent outstanding on her home since she first went on rent strike against internment in 1971. She heard good news – her rent had been more than paid up and she might even get a rebate.

'The thing about Betty Williams is, she just loves being a housewife. I never saw her happier than when she arrived in home and saw her children. She would make herself a cup of tea, then fly round the house cleaning it. When it was spotless and people came round to eat dinner with her, that's when I saw her happiest, sitting by her own fire with a cup of tea in her hand . . . it's desperate to see the state she's in now, even if she did always have a sharp tongue. She was a bit of a high liver, I suppose. Thank God I got out of the Peace People when I did. They nearly destroyed me too.'

The woman who spoke, Margaret Watson, resigned from the Executive of the Peace Movement in June 1977, less than a year after it began.

When I called to see Betty Williams, in March 1980, her house was indeed spotless. She sat by the fire and produced two cups of tea, launching into the easy intimacy for which she was famed among the media who used haunt her house in the halcyon days of 1976. There were no other journalists present on this occasion. Her telephone, once constantly engaged, rang once while I was there.

As we sat chatting her sixteen-year-old son came in from school. Her eight-year-old daughter was being fetched by the live-in housekeeper. 'Ralph used to be away all the time as a merchant seaman. Then I took off as a Peace Leader. It's been hard on the children and I'm glad to be back with them now'.

The framed photographs and citations on one wall of the comfortable room told the story of the last three and a half years. She and Mairead in Oslo receiving the Nobel award: she and Mairead in Rome in an audience with the Pope; she and Mairead and Ciaran receiving the Carl Von Ossietsky Prize from the Berlin Branch of the International League for Human Rights; the Variety Club of Great Britain's award for courage at its Woman of the Year ceremony in Leeds; a doctorate from Yale University, America; an invitation from the Royal Household to attend the Queen Elizabeth Jubilee reception aboard the royal yacht Britannia in Belfast Lough, on the sixth anniversary of the introduction of internment. The invitation was for 'Mrs. Betty Williams and Mr. Williams'.

She did not want to talk about the split in the movement. 'The night I resigned I came back and sat by the fire and relaxed for the first time in years'. Her daughter arrived in home and she invited me to join them on a trip to the seaside resort of Newcastle, Co. Down, a few miles away, where Ralph, who now lives there, had been taking the child for riding lessons.

'I don't own both these cars', she volunteered in the driveway. 'That one belongs to Ralph. He leaves it here when he goes away on his ship'. The Volvo which she drove was relatively new. 'We always had a big car in this family. Now I'm driving all over the country I need my own car to get me there, quickly, safely, and without leaving me exhausted. I suppose you'll want to know about me fur coat. Well, I was going to Norway to get the Nobel award and the eyes of the world were on me as a representative of Northern Ireland. Christ, did people expect me to arrive in a duffle coat?'

As we approached the coast Betty burst into song. 'Where the mountains of Mourne sweep down to the sea'. She knew all the words. The New Zealand woman told me how she had formed a branch of the Peace People there in 1977, and come over in 1978 to see things for herself. 'I came for two weeks and stayed with the movement for a year. Money was coming from New Zealand for the movement. Money was going from the movement to the Third World. I resigned'. She did not want to talk about the split.

We saw the child safely into the riding stables and went to a nearby inn. 'I used to live in Newcastle you know', Betty said over a hot whiskey. 'Ralph was away a lot and I looked at the tree in the yard and thought I'll be up there soon, like a monkey, if I don't do something. So I went back to work, driving into Belfast every day to do dogsbody for a firm of directors'. She had worked all her life, and supported Ralph in the early years when he was studying for his master's ticket. He was an Englishman from Cheshire, and a Methodist, and she married him when she was nineteen. There was no religious problem for Betty, who was born a Catholic in Andersonstown. Her grandfather was a Protestant, a socialist and a Republican from the Tiger Bay in Belfast. Her father became a Catholic shortly before his own marriage to a Catholic. Ralph stayed with the religion he was born into.

'We got married in Bermuda in 1963 and I took a job with Bell Telephones. Then we came back to England for a few years, then to Belfast in 1969, then Newcastle, then back to Belfast', to the middle class suburb of Finaghy. 'I got a job as a waitress in the Dunadri Inn, at night, very posh it was. One time I served dinner to William Whitelaw. That was two jobs I had, one by day and one by night, and my sister looked after the children. Mind you, those days were a walkover compared with the job I've done with the Peace People. You know that story, if it's Tuesday it must be New York. Jesus, I didn't know if it was Tuesday or Wednesday, America or Italy. Hotel rooms look the same the world over.'

The April 1977 issue of the movement's newspaper, *Peace by Peace,* recorded that Betty was in North America, scheduled to address 88 meetings over eighteen days, across Canada and the USA.

Her marriage, she said, was troubled long before she became famous. 'It happens to other people, and then it happened to us. We've been through the bad patches, scoring points off one another; but now you could say we're decent enough with each other. That's Ralph's house over there, look', she pointed to a neat bungalow on a hill. He was paying £100 a month support for the children, she said, 'but naturally it's up to me to pay the main bills. I don't go in for alimony anyway, and God knows I've always been independent.'

Her £38,000 share of the Nobel money hadn't stretched that far. 'It's been two and a half years now, and by the time you pay this and that . . . ' She had put a kitchen extension on her house, bought the fur coat and the car, supported her family, paid a succession of housekeepers 'and then there was all the travel abroad. All my fares and hotels were paid of course, but you don't arrive over there in rags, do you? And you have to entertain the people you meet. I stood me rounds. I didn't do that Paddy poor mouth, I was an ambassadress for Northern Ireland, and I kept up our image.'

She had also given a lot away, 'but you can't start saying who you gave it to. If people want to come forward and say so, well and good . . . ' She expected that some money would come now from lecture tours, 'though there's fewer invitations than in the beginning, of course. I'll soon be spending a week with Amnesty in Canada, but that's free, naturally. Maybe I could get a job in PR – or would that be a disgrace to the Nobel award? I mean to say, I can hardly waitress again, with the medal round my neck. Jesus Christ, I'd be like a freak show'.

She hadn't seen Anne Maguire for three years. 'I was the only one saw her and her three wanes crushed against the railings by that car, and we used to talk about it, and then it got so we dreaded meeting each other, so we didn't'. The death of Anne was a culmination of 'six terrible months . . I've hardly worked for peace since last September. I was coming as close as it was possible to come to a nervous breakdown'.

We parted on her doorstep in Belfast, and I went off to meet Mairead Corrigan, who was selling the movement paper, *Peace by Peace*, that night.

Six months before, in September 1979, while she was on a speaking tour of Germany, Ciaran McKeown had requested a private meeting with the outgoing Executive of the Peace People, to talk about what her he termed 'the private life of Betty Williams'. He went before them with the expressed support of Mairead Corrigan and Peter Mc Lachlan, and none of them told or attempted to tell Williams what they were doing.

Betty, Mairead and Ciaran had resigned from the Executive previously and had just announced that they intended to stand for re-election to it.

'We were concerned about the pressures Betty was undergoing' McKeown told me, 'and we wanted to help her'. He did not at first tell the Executive anything about her that they did not already know. She had publicly stated in the press that she was separated from her husband. Her name had appeared, they already knew, in

Stubbs Gazette, as owing £5,000 to a bank. She had gone guarantor in this sum to a man who subsequently reneged on his debt and left the country. Nor was this her only act of charity, they knew.

The Executive were sympathetic. There was nothing they could or should criticize. McKeown then revealed to them something which, he told me, 'shocked and horrified them'. He told them that the damage done to credibility by the 'mishandling of the Nobel award money' was the sole responsibility of Betty Williams – it was she who made the decision to keep the money, he said, and Mairead Corrigan had no option but to follow suit, to avoid a rift in the movement.

After that night, Betty Williams' standing within the Executive was considerably undercut. McKeown, Corrigan and McLachlan subsequently paid a late night visit to her home to dissuade her from her avowed intention to stand for Chairwomanship of the incoming new Executive. Though she topped the poll and McKeown came near to the bottom, she submitted to their advice, accepted election as a member and withdrew into herself, visible only on overseas trips. To the rank and file it appeared that Betty was lukewarm in her participation locally.

'We suggested to her that she adopt a low profile', McKeown said, explaining the nocturnal visit to her. 'She was living in an unreal world, and not involved in the day to day work of the movement. She wanted more development of local groups, for example, but she never took part in it'. He agreed that she had not been asked to do so, nor had she ever refused an invitation to speak in the North. 'But then she wasn't available. I was even knocking on more doors than she was'. I suggested to him that this seemed reasonable, given that she was a Nobel laureate on whom many international demands were made, while he was not. He replied that all Peace People were expected to do work in the North.

'Here was a lady who never had anything before', he said, 'and suddenly she's a Nobel laureate. That's very hard to adjust to . . . I would have said that by the October elections last year Betty did not rate the description of Peace Leader. The nature of her tours in the United States showed that she was unclear in her judgements, and Betty's prestige as a Peace Leader was a big factor in fund raising . . .'

The funds, of course, were no longer flooding in, as foreigners looked for more than mere rhetoric about peace. Betty's dismissal of Irish Americans as 'third generation leprechauns', when they questioned her campaign against the Provos, did not help the flow. Her tours of Germany, however, were more successful. Together with Peter McLachlan and her close friend Christabel Bielenberg, of the Southern Movement for Peace, she formed in 1979 what came to be known as the German connection, with a trust fund in that country which aimed at helping all movements for peace in Ireland. The promise of substantial German funding for the almost bankrupt Northern peace people, who had not sufficient money for 1980, led directly to the split on the night of 7 February, of this year. The movement was virtually broke and needed the money; the Germans, however, attached strings to the proposed gift.

The financial affairs of the Community of the Peace People have been a source of puzzlement and contention, both within and without, virtually since its inception. In fact, the Community as such has controlled scarcely a single penny of the foreign funding.

In November 1976 the people of Norway collected £202,684.91 which they donated to Betty Williams and Mairead Corrigan as a consolation prize, since it was too late to award them the Nobel Peace Prize for that year. An additional £9,000 was received from Germany and from Trusts and individuals. The two women announced that the entire sum of £217,000, which included bank interest of £5,800, would go into a Northern Ireland Trust Fund, which was set up by Ciaran McKeown in March 1977.

When it was discovered that a charitable Trust could not give money to potentially profit-making institutions such as the small industries McKeown wished to aid, a seperate company called Peace by Peace Ltd., was set up by him. The entire collection was paid into this company, which promptly lent is all to the Trust, reserving the right to claim it back as and when needed for industrial projects.

The directors of the company were the same as the trustees of the Trust, and included people who were not members of the peace people. McKeown was Chairman of both company and trust. The trust was to operate as a completely separate body from the Community of the Peace People, made up of local groups, whom McKeown thought should be self-financing, although preference was to be given by the Trust to projects which the Community organised or supported; the priorities of the Peace People's Assembly and the Executive would have 'profound influence on the decisions of the Trustees'.

After the original account was opened, money continued to flow in from the original fund-raising group in Norway, from individuals, from speaking tours given by Betty and Mairead, until more than three hundred thousand pounds were in the coffers. The vast bulk of this money was controlled by either the Trust or the Company. Some was paid into separate accounts which the Trust opened and earmarked for special purposes. Money from the Ford Foundation subsidised the movement newspaper *Peace by Peace,* editor Ciaran McKeown; money from the Norwegian group subsidized a University of Peace in Achill, directed by McKeown, which opened in the summer of 1978. He taught the history of non-violent protest in the nineteenth century, in Ireland, to 24 students whom he selected himself.

Nearly one hundred thousand pounds was given in grants and loans to youth and community centres and welfare work. £50,000 was spent in buying the Peace House on the Lisburn Road. The rest went on salaries and administration expenses of the House.

In October 1979 Peter McLachlan, Chairman of the Peace People Community, announced that the Community would have to fund itself, since there was less than £50,000 cash remaining in the Trust. The Community, which had raised £4,000 in Northern Ireland in 1979, would require £80,000 for 1980 if it was to remain in operation.

In November 1979, McKeown put himself on three months notice as the £8,000 per year director of the Trust. He had previously resigned as Chairman and trustee of it in May 1978 in order to qualify for a salary, but he remained on as Chairman of the Company in technical control of all monies.

In January 1980 McKeown announced that there would soon be a redefinition of Peter McLachlan's £8,000 a year job as projects manager employed by the Company, since there was no longer money available for such industrial projects. Future salaried staff would be at nominal wages for active 'retired' people and young postgraduates wanting to give a year or two of service.

On 7 February, 1980, the night of the mass resignations,

Peter McLachlan arrived with a detailed report of the proposed German funding. The Germans had expressed dissatisfaction with McKeown's dual role as chairman of the Company and editor of a paper which was heavily subsidized. They specified that all monies donated by them would have to be used for charitable, practicable purposes, to be vetted by Christabel Bielenberg, and could not be used for either the newspaper or pressure groups. McKeown's pressure campaign for justice, particularly on the H-Blocks, (which McLachlan supported), would not, obviously, qualify for such funding. McLachlan's practical projects, and by implication, McLachlan's salary, did qualify.

The meeting began as stormily as it ended. It opened with an announcement that three peace groups had sent letters demanding McKeown's resignation. McKeown proposed that the agenda be suspended to discuss the matter, declaring, 'There will be resignations on this table before the night is over'.

Betty Williams promptly handed in hers and went home. The lines of battle were drawn between those in the Executive who supported McKeown's evocation 'May the peace of Christ disturb you', particularly on matters of justice, and those who supported McLachlan's emphasis on practical reconciliation rather than disturbance. McKeown felt that McLachlan's projects in industry, housing and youth clubs were getting undue priority among the peace people. 'There was far too much attention, energy and resources being put into projects that could be done by other agencies', he told me.

McLachlan felt that McKeown's insistence on total support for special status for H-Block prisoners did not allow puzzled members to pursue understanding at their own pace. They wondered if this, plus the call for dismantling emergency legislation, meant tacit support for the Provos and withdrawal of support for the security forces, whom many saw as upholders of law and order.

Mairead Corrigan supported McKeown, because, she told me, 'the peace people should refuse to be dictated to by outside organisations who wished to finance us'. By night's end, McLachlan was requested by a majority of two votes, to resign as Chairman of the Peace People, and his employment as Projects Manager was terminated, an action which the Executive later admitted it had no right to do since McLachlan was employed by the independent Company. The Company announced that McLachlan had their support and the stage was set for further confrontation which McLachlan gracefully ended by resigning voluntarily.

He announced as he left the Peace People 'Betty Williams is no saint but I have come to respect her more these last few months'. Mairead Corrigan was appointed Chairwoman in his place.

I met her in the Peace House, on Lisburn Road, shortly after leaving Betty Williams. It was eight o'clock in the evening and some men had arrived in the large red brick manse, a former presbytery, to plan the Junior Football League which the movement organises across the sectarian divide. In the front downstairs room where they gathered, a large painting hung over the fireplace. It showed a long line of poor and wretched people struggling up a hill, their hands outstretched to Mairead Corrigan, who stood on top, smiling joyously, a light around her head. To the left, behind her, moving out of the painting, Anne Maguire, a sad faced woman with spectacles, pushed a baby in a pram, as two children clung to her coat.

Mairead proposed to sell *Peace by Peace* in the Clonard area, near the spot on the Falls Road where she had once been attacked while picketing the offices of Provisional Sinn Fein. A false front tooth bears witness to one of the many blows she has received in her campaign against them. We left the house accompanied by four other people – Alan Senior, Executive member and paid Assistant Editor of *Peace by Peace*; Steve McBride, Executive member and paid Assistant Editor of *Peace by Peace;* Anne Conville, unpaid member of the Executive; and a young boy, the only volunteer from the rank and file of the Peace People. The paper is subsidized yearly by several thousand pounds from the Trust.

We went into Dunmore Street, a poorly lit terraced ghetto, populated mainly by pensioners. When she introduced herself by name on the doorsteps, the old people smiled warmly at Mairead and expressed their regret at the recent death of her sister. When she announced anonymously that she was from the Peace People, they looked at her vaguely in the darkness. As we progressed down the street five sub-teenage boys gathered round us. They were tough, cheerful, excited and extremely cruel. 'Cry, Mairead, cry' they flung the legendary taunt at the woman whose tears had often flowed in television interviews. She was very good with them. She stood there and asked them if they played football and showed them photographs of the young leaguers in the newspapers. They recognised one team and talked to her about it, boasting about their own prowess in the game. Then they became bored.

The eldest boy took a proferred paper from her, tore it up and let the pieces fly away in the cold night wind. They ran away calling, 'how's Betty the teeth?' They returned later as she stood talking with an elderly man who had retired home from England to live with his aged mother. He was a bit lonely, he said. She told him he would find plenty of friends in the Peace House and he said he'd never heard of it. The children started to whack me over the head with a branch torn from a bush in nearby church grounds. Then they ran away again.

A British Army patrol came by on foot. They immediately approached us wanting to know what literature we were selling and on whose behalf. 'We're trying to do you out of a job', Mairead told them cheerfully. 'We support non-violence.' Alan Senior, of the majority tradition, called the troop leader 'sir' and wished them good night. He told me later that he regarded the army as 'a peacekeeping force'; rifles, when carried by the right people, do not represent violence, he said.

In Aranmore Street a teenager on crutches came to the door and was surprised to recognise her. He had hurt his foot in an industrial accident shortly after finishing a jail term for paramilitary activity. Now he expected to return to jail again, as he had been charged with rifling the offices of the SDLP, an old offence, and membership of the Provisional IRA. He wondered if anybody could help him. She gave him a free paper, saying he should call at the Peace House. He laughed and said he wasn't at all sure about doing that. When she heard his name she said 'I used to do a line with your uncle.' 'You must have been hard up', he said. There was warmth between them.

As she moved off the children returned, throwing stones. When the missiles began to find their mark, on her legs and mine, we hurried ignominiously back to the car. A woman called from a lighted doorstep 'Where's Betty, Mairead? Are you looking for more money?'

Steve McBride said it was always Mairead's presence, or Betty's or Ciaran's, that attracted animosity. We drove back to the Peace

House and had tea and biscuits with the football managers and the two women who were in charge of the house that night. They were pleased and surprised to have sold nearly fifty copies of the outdated fortnightly paper – a new issue was due out the following day. The eight page edition which they had just sold contained a full page on the plight of Australian aborigines; a half page on women under Islam; a half page on malnutrition in the Third World; a full page on the advantages of breast over bottle feeding, with specific reference to the Third World; a half page on the difference between cash and the monetary policy of banks, quoting a 1932 reference work; a full back page on the junior football league; a half page on youth clubs; and scattered photographs of the peace people Funline group at a barn dance.

The front page dealt with the split. 'The entire story of what has been happening may someday be written', it said. 'What appears in this edition is as much as the Peace People Executive considers proper . . . at long last the Executive has assumed its responsibilities and made it clear internally and externally that the Peace People is now a democratic organisation'. They had recently been 'bedevilled by constant talk of differing approaches' but this was now resolved and major areas of exciting work had been shared out. 'These include such items as European invitations to hold political dialogue meetings in hospitable circumstances and several youth camps'. The Executive, it said, had been 'too long dependent on the founding leaders for funds and representation'.

Another front page story announced that a British expert on yoga had given a talk on yoga in the Peace House. At the bottom of the page, in heavy black type, Betty Williams was quoted as saying she would be concentrating on family responsibilities. She 'told Ciaran McKeown "You and Mairead have all my love and support for the future of the movement".' The paper did not express a single word of support for Betty. Nor did it mention the apology which the Executive had publicly made to McLachlan, exonerating him from any question of financial fraud.

Before this edition was printed, Mairead Corrigan went to Betty Williams' home at two o'clock in the morning asking to see her. The housekeeper pleaded that Betty was exhausted. At 4 am the Williams household was again awakened as Mairead returned with Ciaran McKeown and Joe Johnston, press relations officers of the Executive. Mairead went up to Betty's room and woke her. They came downstairs and Betty was asked if she would pose before the media at 11 am that morning for a photograph of her, Mairead and Ciaran together.

'By eleven tomorrow this whole thing will be over', Ciaran said. 'There'll be no more talk about a split between us in the movement'.

She refused, and flew off on a lecture tour to America, from where she issued a statement expressing love for Mairead only. 'I did not express support for the movement' she said, adding 'Women of Ireland, I love you.'

Ciaran McKeown issued a reply. 'Betty is often inexcusably inaccurate'.

Mairead Corrigan invited me to lunch at the Peace House, where members take turns at preparing meals for each other and for visitors who drop in. On this occasion she herself prepared the mince pie. The all male company, apart from myself and Mairead, included Sammy McClure of the UDA and his teenage son, another member of the UDA, and a man from Comhaltas Ceoltoiri Eireann. Also present were Alan Senior, another elderly retired accountant who handles the movement's books, and a young American law student who is advising the Peace People on Northern Ireland's emergency legislation.

Sammy talked for a while about his granny, to whose astounded hospital bedside he had brought a friend of his, a Catholic priest. Then the chat turned to modern morality. The Comhaltas man told how he had attended a dinner dance in County Armagh where he was aghast to receive an invitation to throw his door key under the table for a bit of wife swapping. Sam deplored this, though he was not puritan about sex 'as the evidence, my son here, shows'. He was glad we had progressed beyond Old Testament restrictions, where people were instructed how to beget, by wearing in bed full length garments that contained apertures for the appropriate mingling of the appropriate parts. They moved on to unmarried mothers, and Mairead steered the discussion to love, observing that people today seemed more genuinely and openly affectionate in their relationships with each other.

Later, in her simply furnished upstairs office, she showed me the volume of international correspondence she has to deal with. She was just then writing to her contact in the Vatican to try and arrange an audience with the Pope for Adolfo Esquivel, the Latin

American non-violent leader whom she and Betty had nominated for the 1978 Nobel Peace Prize. She had met him in Argentina last September when she went over there to work on behalf of missing prisoners.

The Pope, she said, was the most impressive of all the world leaders she had met, and she had asked him if he agreed that there is no such thing as a just war, pointing out that early Christians were actually forbidden to become soldiers. 'His reply saddened me. He said he couldn't say all wars were unjust because there are sometimes different circumstances.'

He had laughed when she kissed him goodbye on the cheek and said that her father wanted to know if he could have a contract for the Vatican windows. Her father had worked as a window cleaner cum ice-cream salesman before retirement. Her mother had worked in a fruit shop, in a room above which Mairead was born, in the Falls Road, in 1944. 'That's the shop Paisley marched on in 1964 because the Officials had made it their election headquarters and stuck a tricolour in the window.'

The Corrigan family, comprising six girls and two boys, had long since moved to Andersonstown. One of her sisters had been killed in a car accident in 1969 at the same spot where Anne's children were killed in 1976. Two married sisters were now rearing families in Belfast, one worked for RTE in Dublin, a married brother was a bus driver in New Zealand, and the youngest brother, aged twenty-three, an architect, stayed at home with her parents.

When the Peace Movement started she soon found herself obliged to leave both her job and her parent's home. 'They were grieving over the children and the press were besieging me day and night and through the night. So I packed a suitcase and stayed with a girlfriend for about six weeks, though I was spending most of the time in Betty's house'. She got herself a flat then, and stayed there fairly constantly for over a year, until Anne returned from New Zealand where she had emigrated in search of release from grief. 'It didn't work and when they came home I stayed with her for a while, trying to help'. She returned to her flat after the Maguires employed a young housekeeper. Anne was receiving psychiatric care and had made two attempts at suicide. In the months before Anne's death, Mairead was again moving between her flat and the Maguire household. Now she lives there semi-permanently.

Before the Peace Movement upturned her life she had led a regular, anonymous existence, working as secretary to the managing director of a brewery, and doing welfare work for the Legion of Mary. She had represented the Legion in 1974 at the World Council of Churches in Thailand, travelling over with Harold Good, a Methodist Minister from the Shankill, who is now a director of the Peace Trust. As a legionaire she worked with the handicapped children in Anderstown, moving into welfare when internment began. She used visit Long Kesh every weekend, and spent time with the families of the prisoners. Her own family was not untouched by the troubles. An aunt was burned out of her house in Norfolk Street by loyalists. Her teenage brother was taken away for questioning by the British Army and she could not find out where he was.

She understood, she said, why people were driven to joining the Provos. She had gone with a bouquet of roses to sympathize with Kathleen Lennon, and visited the wife of the young man who was wounded in the car with Danny. If her campaign for an end to violence had since been aimed mostly at the Provos, it was because, she said, 'the loyalists who assassinated weren't openly identifiable, and they called for a ceasefire within nine months, anyway'. (The Shankill Butchers operated in the early months of the Peace Movement). She had never picketed British Army headquarters 'because there was never a black and white case where you could be a hundred per cent sure that they had deliberately killed an innocent civilian'. (Twelve-year-old Majella O'Hare was shot dead by the British troops on the day that Betty and Mairead held their first peace rally on Finaghy Road).

Even now, four months after she'd started, 'I know so little about non-violence and how to handle it. Ciaran knows all about Gandhi and Luther King and pacifism. You'd need to talk to him about it.' She seemed genuinely perplexed. 'I haven't had the advantage of a university education that Ciaran has had. I left school at fifteen. I started going to the Polytechnic last autumn to do a BA in history, politics and philosophy but that's been interrupted with looking after the children.' Ciaran was giving them education classes now in media training and non-violence, and had been responsible from the start for the philosophy of the movement, 'but the peace-making is so hard, even among peace people'.

In Dungannon last year, where she had spoken of dismantling the Emergency Provisions Act, because repressive laws increased the cycle of violence, 'a woman grabbed me. She was a police widow. Her husband had been killed by the Provos.' The woman thought they needed even more laws against the IRA and was crying in anger and grief. 'I had learned by then to lower my eyes and take it. The woman walked away after a while, then she came back and said "I'm sorry".'

She recalled the night the three of them had gone to Turf Lodge in October 1976 where a protest meeting had been called by community leaders after the British Army killed a child with a plastic bullet. The crowd turned on them, physically assaulting them, and they were forced to seek refuge in a nearby church. 'I had to shout to make myself heard, and I knew even while I was doing it that the shouting lifted the anger up . . . one woman grabbed my arm and said "My husband's in Long Kesh. I don't know when he'll get out." She pointed at my leather coat and said "Haven't you done well for yourself?" At that time the movement was only seven weeks old, and I'd left my job and wasn't getting any money.'

She had gone on salary from the Peace People, at £5,000 a year in January 1977. When the Nobel was received in November, she and Betty had come off salary, supporting themselves. 'I also gave about half of the money away'. She had given her old car to relatives, bought a new two door Skoda and some clothes. 'But I has my half musquash coat since 1974'. She now has no life insurance, had not stamped her own cards since leaving the brewery and hadn't 'thought about a pension'.

She said, wistfully, that she didn't expect now ever to have the marriage and children of her own that she would have liked. 'It's been hard to keep up the personal relationships I had before all this started, but Betty kept me going tremendously, and I have a special relationship with Ciaran and his wife Marian'.

She had been sustained over the last few years by her faith in Christ; she goes to Mass and communion every day, and visits Lough Derg once a year. 'You could say I'm having a love affair with Jesus. When things are bad I go to church and sit there with him. At the worst moment I heard God say to me "I have given you something tough. You'll have to bear it", and I knew that finally it all comes back to being on your own, no matter who is around you, husband, children or friends'.

It was right for Betty to leave the movement, she said. 'She felt herself that she had to get her own personal life in order, and she had to find money to support her family'. It was Betty who decided to keep the Nobel money, she said. Mairead's first television reaction, when she said her mother needn't worry about Mairead not having a husband to keep her 'was a joke, that's all. Later I said that some of the money would have to go to the Third World. Betty then wanted it all to go to the Movement'.

Shortly after the Nobel award was announced, in October 1977, a meeting was held in Betty's house to discuss the disposal of the money that came with it. Present at it were Betty, Mairead, Ciaran and Max Magee, administrator of the Peace House and an expert in para psychology. Magee, Ciaran told me, came to see the Peace Leaders early in 1977 'and he noticed the special relationship between the three of us. He suggested that we be freed from routine duties to explore this and he took over the Peace House'.

Magee is now principal of the College of Psychic Studies in London. 'We had planned', said McKeown, 'that the money would provide each of the three of us with the £5,000 a year salary we were then taking from the Movement. Some of it was to go to educational projects, which I was to direct, and some would go to the Third World project which each of us would adopt. When we walked in the door Betty announced that she had projects of her own in mind, and wanted to keep her share for them. She didn't agree with what we had planned'.

I asked him if he had advised her on the repercussions of keeping personal control of the money.

'No, I didn't. When Betty has her mind made up, that's that. You don't understand the effects of a Nobel prize on a person . . . it's like a lay canonisation'.

The canonisation process had begun a year earlier within 24 hours of the deaths of the Maguire children, when Betty Williams was made a press celebrity. It resulted from the convergence of two historical phenomena – modern media techniques and the liberation of women – was fuelled by the worldwide threat to parliamentarians of armed guerilla movements, (particularly in Germany), and was sustained locally by a genuine sense of war weariness.

In August 1976, despair, futility and violence pervaded the hot summer streets of Belfast. Convention talks among the North's politicians had just failed; Ulster was in a political limbo, ruled directly and remotely from the British mainland; there was warfare involving the British Army, the Provisional IRA and myriad loyalist armies.

On Tuesday, 10 August, there was widespread violence in Catholic areas as demonstrators commemorating the fifth anniversary of the introduction of internment burnt vehicles, smashed shop windows and set up roadblocks. At two in the afternoon the British Army opened fire on a vehicle which they believed to be the get-away car from a previous ambush. The car contained two young IRA volunteers. Danny Lennon, at the wheel, died in the hail of bullets, the car went out of control and smashed into Anne Maguire and her three children.

Betty Williams, returning by car from Anderstown where she had visited her crippled mother, saw what happened next. 'The baby shot out of the pram, into the air and bounced off the windscreen. The woman was crushed against the railings. So was a young child. I saw a young boy being dragged under the mudguard'. She stopped and went back to the scene. There was blood and confusion and horror. She went home, thought about it, and the other violent deaths she had witnessed, and decided to organise a petition 'calling on the gunmen to stop'.

Accompanied by her only sister she went out that night knocking on doors. Women who had been trying unsuccessfully to prevent what they saw as the senseless destruction of Anderstown, followed her like a Pied Piper and the Peace Movement was unofficially born.

Kathleen Lennon that afternoon had visited her mother, delivering bread, because she knew the Falls Road shops would be shut. As she waited afterwards in the street for a black taxi, her sister arrived in a car driven by a man whom she recognised as a member of the Provisional Sinn Fein. They offered her a lift home; on the way they told her of Danny's death.

Mairead Corrigan on that day was driving home from a holiday in Achill. She arrived home late and knew that something was wrong because the house was lit up. Her aunt was coming down the garden path. 'Mairead, all Anne's children are dead', the woman said.

Ciaran McKeown, on that day, was painting the windows of his house, which had been petrol bombed the previous year. (He suspected left wing paramilitaries because a book on Lenin was found nearby). He received a telephone call from an Irish Press colleague, telling him that an unspecified number of children had been killed in a suspected shoot-out, and that the evening shift would be a difficult one. McKeown started making phone calls.

On Wednesday, 11 August, Mairead Corrigan, in the company of Anne's husband Jackie, visited her sister who lay unconscious in hospital after neuro surgery. They arranged for the removal of the bodies of two of the children. 'You can come back and sign for the baby later. He'll be dead by then', a young policeman told them. The funeral, proposed for Tuesday, was delayed.

On Thursday morning, 12 August, Mairead went to the offices of UTV and said, 'I want to go on television'. The interview was filmed on the roof of the building and broadcast in the evening. She was in tears and she said she wanted the violence to stop. That night she heard that Betty Williams was organising a rally to call for just that. 'I rang her up and asked her to join my family in the Church on Friday for the funeral'. She then went on to the home of Kathleen Lennon.

'She sat on my sofa with a bunch of roses she had brought me, and we were both upset', Kathleen Lennon recalls. 'She asked me if I thought Danny knew what he was doing when he joined the IRA. I told her he had just come out of jail after serving a sentence since 1972, and that my other son had been interned and was now serving a sentence, and Danny was determined to work for his country. She told me to keep that thought with me, never to let anyone take it away from me that Danny was proud of his country. Then she went to America and said the IRA were terrorists. I never met her again. I didn't want to. Her sister Anne came to see me on the second anniversary of all the deaths in 1978. She wanted me to come and visit her sometimes in her own home, but she said she understood why I couldn't, because Mairead Corrigan was staying with them at that time'.

On Friday evening, 13 August, after the funeral, both Betty and Mairead went to UTV to take part in a Telefis Eireann broadcast on the burgeoning phenomena that still had no name. They arrived too late for the programme, which went ahead with Paddy Devlin and Ciaran McKeown, and met the two men coming out of a lift. Introductions were made. 'I had never met Ciaran before', Mairead told me, 'but I congratulated him on a series of articles he had written about integrated education in the North'. (McKeown's father, a headmaster, had clashed with Bishop Philbin on the matter and Ciaran had been debarred by the Bishop from entering his father's school as a reporter. His father was forced to retire early).

McKeown told the women that he thought something big was about to result from the rally Betty had planned, and offered to help. Later that night, he told me, he dropped round to Betty's house, found she wasn't there, and left his name and home telephone number with her only sister.

The turnout next day, Saturday 14 August, surpassed and confounded all expectations, except those of McKeown, who told me he had 'sensed it would be so'. Thousands of people, mainly women, simply came and stood and shared an undefined hope. Protestant and Catholic women rushed to embrace each other, crossing the sectarian divide in scenes unprecedented in the long turbulent history of Northern Ireland. There were no speeches, no analysis of why they were there, or what they were looking for. The heart has its reasons, which reason may not know.

Over the weekend the foreign media followed the Williams household, asking Betty and Mairead to pronounce on every issue that had ever affected Northern Ireland. In desperation and confusion, they rang McKeown constantly seeking his advice, relaying his answers. 'They were calling me so often I suggested we meet and talk', McKeown told me and he arranged to meet them on Tuesday 17 August, in the presbytery of the Church of St Michael of the Archangel, from where the children had been buried. By that time a flood of mail had engulfed Betty's house – letters, telegrams, money donations. 'It was like monopoly', she told me. 'I'd open one envelope after another and out would come funny money, coloured bits of foreign paper. A Methodist woman had called, looking to help and I made her treasurer on the spot'.

The three met, that night, and Betty handed McKeown for perusal a declaration about peace which she had written, which ended with a call on gunmen to get out. McKeown told me he found her statement 'simplistic, naive, one sided on the matter of violence, and even violent in tone'. He took a page from

Mairead's jotter and wrote there and then, the Declaration of the Peace People.

In the opening line he addressed it to 'the world, from this movement of peace', and he recorded a series of simple aspiration for a just and peaceful society, that could be imbibed, like custard, by anybody, with the exception of line seven, which rejected 'the use of bomb and bullet and all techniques of violence'.

They agreed to work together from then on, with McKeown initially in the background. He was still a staff journalist and he wished to avoid speculation, he told me, 'that an undoubtedly spontaneous movement was being manipulated by a person of my background'. McKeown was a former student leader and civil rights activists, with vaguely left leanings, who had stood for Dail Eireann in 1969 as an independent, collecting 154 votes.

They discussed, he said, the sexist nature of the term Peace Women, and they decided henceforth to refer to themselves as Peace People.

The media, aware even then of McKeown's influence, were not interested in another bearded Irish male. They seized shamelessly on the Belfast women in those first four weeks, projecting Williams as super housewife and Corrigan as saintly spinster. Feminism however was an issue that attracted serious world wide attention at that time, and the elevation of token women regularly occurred. On September 17, 1976, Irish newspapers recorded that Williams and Corrigan had been jointly nominated for the 1976 Nobel Prize by the chairman of the Norwegian Christian People's Party, Mr Kaare Kristiansen, and the President of the West German Lower House, Frau Anne Marie Renger. The call was echoed by the German branch of the World Council of Mothers of all Nations. The Peace Movement was then thirty four days old. The Prize was to be awarded in October. In the event, the nominations were made too late and they received the award in October 1977.

None of this is to deny that the two women who called for an end to violence raised a heartfelt response in the war-torn community of Northern Ireland. The response, indeed, was immediate and massive; on the first exulting marches no one asked to see the blueprint. Ciaran McKeown was busy writing it, and his pamphlet *The Price of Peace,* appeared in late September. Meanwhile, there were the heady rallies. A Southern Movement for

Peace sprang up, holding rallies to coincide with the ones that were being organised in Northern Ireland and Great Britain. From September through to December it seemed as if, on successive Saturdays, the entire peoples of the two islands were on the move behind Williams, Corrigan and McKeown.

Ciaran had planned the marches, spreading Betty and Mairead evenly over the two countries. One of them would be in England every second Saturday. There were summonses from abroad to go there and tell their tale. The summonses were hard to resist; there was the chance to re-awaken international interest in a country and a problem that had seemed to be boringly intractable. There was an opportunity of foreign funding for the movement; and there was the very human lure of travel and excitement for three people of relatively colourless backgrounds. Mairead's trip to Thailand, Betty's year in Bermuda, Ciaran's year as President of the Union of Students in Ireland – these brief bursts in the sun were as nothing to the invitations that now flowed in, to travel as media stars and the darlings of foreign governments.

For Ciaran McKeown, a 32-year-old local journalist, who had been stationed in the North for the previous six year, it was a sunburst beyond his wildest dreams. He provided the world's media with weighty thoughts on peace as a supplement to the human interest stories on the peace women. His pamphlet *The Price of Peace,* which he published and paid for on his own initiative, represented, he said in a forward, 'the thinking which has largely guided the Movement of the Peace People'. It suggested, he wrote, 'an attempt to create a society closer to the tenets of Christianity than perhaps anything since the days immediately after the death of Christ himself'. He was confident to tell his dream in public, he recorded, 'because I am a professional communicator, as well as a philosopher by qualification, and a pacifist by conviction'. In the third reprint, (the pamphlet sold like hotcakes on the marches) he wrote of his own thinking 'some (usually outside Northern Ireland) have made such gratifying observations that (sic) it is the clearest statement of the pacifist position since Gandhi'.

The pamphlet did indeed attract the attention of the foreign editor of a right wing Norwegian newspaper, who read it and decided to launch a campaign for funds for the Peace Movement, to compensate for the fact that it was too late to give Mairead and

Betty the Nobel award. Since the Norwegian fund was arguably the golden egg that choked the fledgling movement, it is worth exploring here the ideas which McKeown had put forward.

'No one is going to come dowm from the mountain with a new set of tablets', he wrote, but he 'presumed to offer some guidance'. He was convinced that the people of Northern Ireland could not only create a brave new world, but give a powerful example to such as Lebanon, South Africa and people under totalitarian regimes – 'another way forward for the human race will have been proved possible'.

He recommended self-help for the North, which was in unfair competition with larger industrial states, by concentrating on arts and crafts. The Swiss, he wrote, had watchmaking. Northern Ireland could start with the men in jail who made money from leathercrafts. Work could be provided by restoring the bombed houses that seperated the warring ghettos.

He hinted at a federation of the British Isles, in which there would be a new Northern Irish identity, distinct 'but not separate from any of them', and sketches of the government which would emerge from this new identity. Community associations, co-operatives, private enterprises, trade unions 'and so on', would emerge as competing groups for the central authority of this new democracy. 'What is certain', he declared, 'is that the old parties are as good as dead in their present forms'.

The news media should rethink its role – 'the badness of violence is so repetitive as to be scarcely newsworthy' – and *Peace by Peace* should quickly establish itself as a key organ of the new genre, stimulating 'pacifist and near pacifist thinking'. (McKeown had launched the movement paper in September). In a chapter on sexism, he urged that women should have 'a couple of nights out in the pub or whatever, with a certain amount of pocket money'. Women, he said 'appear to have grasped much more surely and intuitively the real fundamental change in our Northern Irish situation. Men will follow when it is spelled out more clearly'.

He concluded his 32 page pamphlet with a suggestion that those who were sometimes unjustly maligned 'as the fur coat do-gooders' should twin with a place in Latin America and help them establish their own peaceful society. 'We will move all the more quickly towards our own destiny if we begin now to work for peace elsewhere'.

Gunnar Borrovik, foreign editor of the *Federelandsvennen,* read this and launched a campaign for funds. *Peace by Peace* published an article which explained what happened after that. 'At first it was only the right wing papers that appealed for donations – the left wing didn't know how to react at all'. The fund halted at £15,000 and then took off again after a televised interview with Williams and Corrigan called 'Two Women for Peace', mounting to £202,000, which surpassed the original aim of reaching a sum equivalent to the Nobel money. 'I also suspect', the correspondent wrote 'that people were motivated by an urge to take the Norwegian peace thing into their own hands for once, rather than leave it to a group of politicians to honour the likes of Henry Kissinger – a sense of shame undoubtedly obtains'. The three went to Norway in November to accept the money. The people there 'may have fallen in love with sweet Miss Corrigan but the impression that remains is that of a cool balanced head of the man in the background'. The article recorded Norwegian amazement at the trio's naievety in believing that they could offer an example to the whole world, recommending 'a little less of the crusading spirit and a bit more humility'.

When they left the formality of the town hall where the presentation was made 'the visitors visibly changed; they were clearly in their element as they stood at the head of the 10,000 slogan chanting marchers . . . almost totally dependent on the emotional factor . . . would they dare to talk of the common plight of small nations to a crowd in Woodvale Park, Belfast?'

Betty said the money would be spent on a recreation centre for children. Ciaran set up a Trust Fund to dispose of it. In the formative first two years of the Peace People he was Chairman of the Trust, the Company and the Movement, editor of the paper and the author of the pamphlets which explained movement thinking.

Even as they were in Norway, in November, things had already turned sour. The H-Block blanket protest had started in September and the marches in Catholic areas met fierce opposition from Provisional supporters, angered at the movement's concentration on the IRA while the Shankill Butchers' assassination campaign was virtually ignored by it. (The UDA, of which some of the Butchers were members, had publicly welcomed the Peace March up the Shankill Road. Their offer to provide security for it was, however, turned down). When the British government lifted the ban that had been imposed since Bloody Sunday 1972 against Irish demonstrations in Trafalgar Square, in order that the Peace People and Joan Baez speak there, there were suggustions that the government were exploiting Peace activities as a smokescreen for their own political inertia. The Queen's mention of the Peace Women in her Christmas address lent support to this view.

But the masses who flocked to the peace banner remained inspired. Margaret Watson from Belfast who joined the Movement in those early days described to me what it was like, 'I was watching television in September and I saw Betty Williams. I sat up with a shock. For years I had left politics to my husband; I watched his enthusiasm, saw him take part in citizens defence committees, was used to being introduced as his wife, and sat back with nothing to say. When the Peace Movement started, I identified, straight away. I found a place in the vacuum.

'I saw Betty Williams and I thought, "she's just an ordinary housewife like me. If she can speak up, why can't I at least support her". But I thought she was going to tell the gunmen to get out. That was wrong. They were part of our community. I knew that much. They had to be stopped, but we couldn't just fling them out; that was dishonest, and immoral.

'So I sat down that night and wrote a letter, explaining that I thought we had to offer a place also to gunmen, if we really felt peaceful to everybody, and I sent it to her.

'About a week later, in the evening, her husband Ralph arrived at my door and asked me to go to Betty's house. I did. I joined the Peace Movement, in her house, that night, just like that. Ciaran McKeown talked to me about the gunmen staying with us, and he said I was right, and before I knew it I was on the executive, just like that. There were no elections, you just joined, and made up the movement as you went along'.

Her eyes were bright, as she spoke to me in the sitting room of her home, her face animated in the way I have seen many women's faces animated in the first flush of the Womens Liberation Movement in Dublin, when housewives suddenly felt they had a voice.

'We used to meet in the Presbyterian centre and then we moved to the Peace House in the Lisburn Road. It was the most exciting year of my life. I'll never forget them for it, and I'll always thank them for that. I worked morning noon and night for them, and couldn't sleep at night sometimes for the excitement. I'll tell you how busy I was. I came home one evening. I had missed the tea, my husband made it for the three children, and I was reading a Ladybird book to my young son, just before he went to bed, and he pointed to a picture of a vacuum cleaner, and said, "that's the thing Daddy uses about the house". That's how involved I was with the Peace Movement'.

There had been, she said, strong criticism of the Peace Leaders for always being abroad and the makeshift executive had been very sensitive about it. 'Ciaran thought other people should make some of the trips, to ease the criticism and give others some experience. One morning, in January I think it was, the phone rang in the Peace House and someone spoke from Belgium saying they wanted to make Betty and Mairead honorary members of the Union of European Federalists, whoever they were, I hadn't a clue at the time. I told them Betty and Mairead were booked up for foreign travel, and this voice at the other end said "Will you come please?' Me? I told them I was nobody and this voice said, "No, no, you are a member of the Peace Movement, please come".'

Within two weeks she found herself with another female member of the Executive flying to Belgium.

'It was . . . how can I put it? It was like being a film star. I'd been abroad once before, in a camping bag, and worrying about the price of food. But now, here I was, flying, no worry about the fare, they paid it, and they met us on the tarmacadam and presented us with a bouquet of roses each. Then we were swept into a limousine by a member of the Union; he actually owned a big building company, and he came with us into town and showed us to our hotel.

'Well, I can tell you, I would have been content to spend the weekend in the hotel suite alone, it was luxury beyond by wildest dreams. They took us on a tour of the town, all these important business people, and their wives; they were totally charming. I kept wondering if they minded that I wasn't Mairead or Betty, but not once did they make me feel like a second class peace person. It was like we were idols. Members of the Peace Movement, and that was a passport to idolatry.

'When we were presented with medals and scrolls I got up to

read my speech, a little one, that I had prepared in French, then I discovered that the area was Walloon, and French was sacreligious to them, that's how well we were prepared. I read out the declaration of the Peace People instead; there was television and everything in the hall, and some of them actually had tears in their eyes. Of course, in those days, the Peace Declaration actually made me cry; I meant every word of it, I really did'.

She had already been through the peace rallies on the Falls Road and the meeting in Turf Lodge where the leaders were attacked.

'I thought we were going to be killed on the Falls Road. We were marching up to the park, where Anne Maguire, on crutches, just out of hospital, was ready to read out the declaration. As we got near Milltown Cemetery, the Provos started stoning us. The stones and bits of metal were raining down on us; I often wondered since if it was God's intervention that sent us a rainy day, the first march on which there had been bad weather, because our umbrellas saved us. The movement was like that, you really believed God was watching over us. I was terrified, terrified.

'I'd often seen civil rights marches being attacked, on television, but I never knew it was as fearsome as that. And there was poor Anne Maguire, inside the park, up on a platform, alone with a priest, and the Provos between us and her, and her crutches and pins in her legs. I came away from the march convinced of being a pacifist, because you know, you felt you were facing death, from your own people, if you like, that you'd been reared among, and yet I felt love for them, I really did'.

The first split in the movement occured as a result of that march. Ciaran McKeown afterwards wrote an article in the 1977 January edition of the magazine *Fortnight,* which he edited, in which he compared clergymen in the North to 'apostles hiding in the upper room – an image which leapt to mind at the spectacle of Bishop Philbin and Monsignor Mullally lurking behind the gates of Milltown Cemetery when peace marchers were being stoned in the Falls Rally'.

Margaret Watson thought McKeown wrong to so accuse them. 'Poor Philbin was an old man, too old to march anyway, and he had been waiting for us at the top of the Falls'.

As a result of McKeown's article, there were resignations from Tom Conaty, a prominent Belfast lay Catholic and leader of the Anderstown peace branch, demanding an undertaking from the

leaders that they refrain from criticising churches and churchmen.
chmen.

'That's when I first saw how clever Ciaran was', Margaret said.
'Tom Conaty came to see the executive in our headquarters in the
Presbyterian centre, in the upper room, funnily enough, and
presented us with an ultimatum. Well, he was on a loser from the
start, because of course the Peace Movement could not withhold
criticism of churches, where it was merited, and Philbin anyway
was a very rigid Catholic and we weren't feeling all that warm
about him. But it was Ciaran's manoeuvring that night in January
that amazed me.

'He looked Conaty in the eye and said "If you want to complain
about that article you'd better go down the road and speak to the
editor of *Fortnight*". "I am speaking to you, Ciaran", said Tom.
"No you're not. You're speaking to Ciaran McKeown, editor of
Peace by Peace and I have no control over what Ciaran McKeown
of *Fortnight* publishes", Ciaran said. He ran rings around poor
Tom'. Conaty and the Anderstown branch resigned.

Nor was this the first example of McKeown's manoeuvring. He
had announced that a prominent Protestant would be joining the
movement, confounding those who accused the leadership of being Catholic oriented. 'I can tell you I was confounded when
McLachlan arrived one night in October 1976 at a meeting, and
the next thing I heard was Ciaran calling him forward and an-
nouncing him as a member of the Executive. I was shocked. Here
he was, a member of the Unionist Party that had introduced internment and done down Catholics, joining the Executive on his
first night. I went up to him and told him that I hated him. He
asked me to give him a chance and said he was surprised at Ciaran
promoting him like that'. McKeown later appointed McLachlan
Projects Manager of McKeown's Company, with responsibility
for small industrial projects. Betty Williams was also shocked. She
told me she had spoken briefly with McLachlan that first evening
merely to tell him she hated his guts'. In fact McLachlan quickly
won the confidence and trust of the membership including
Williams. 'That was the thing that was really wonderful', said
Watson. 'Protestants and Catholics were talking to each other, actually saying hello'.

While faltering communication were begun, and people were
learning to talk without getting at each other's throats 'things

were going on above our heads that we had no idea about', she said, 'and there was nothing we could have done about them anyway because there were no formal structures until April 1977. There were no rules, really, is the best way to put it'.

Betty Williams had announced that the Peace People were helping ex-paramilitaries to resettle abroad, using an escape route that few in the movement knew about for reasons of security. (£4,000 was spent by the Trust on such resettlements in the first year). Ciaran McKeown had called for the disbandment of the Irish army and co-opted the British peace groups into the Northern Peace Movement saying the Peace People had no geographical limitations and could handle an English branch dealing with racial problems. The movement announced in January 1979 a strategy for peace, based on McKeown's pamphlet, which called for a federation of the British Isles and a Northern model parliament elected from community groups.

'There was one really weird night', said Margaret Watson, 'when he came into the Executive and told us that he had discovered a Third World island, the same size as Ulster, with exactly the same population, and he proposed that we adopt it, send money and advisers to them, and bring them up to the same material level as our own. We voted him down'.

There was confusion among the rank and file about the monies collected from abroad. Northern peace groups, thinking they had access to it, came up with ambitious schemes for using it, offering ideas that ranged from a battered wives home to a portacabin youth centre. The peace movement, McKeown deflected them, should try to be self-sufficient and pay for its own schemes. The Trust Fund, would consider sympathetically applications made to it, both from within and without the peace movement.

In April 1977 the Peace People held an interim spring assembly, at which an ad hoc caretaker committee was elected which would run the movement formally until proper elections were held in October. McKeown was appointed Chairman. He was also Chairman of the Trust and the Company and editor of *Peace by Peace*.

McKeown through his newspaper, made preposterous claims on behalf of the Peace People, which the inexperienced rank and file took at face value. In April, for example, he ran a front page lead story in doubled size heavy black type, written by himself, accompanied by a large photograph of himself, which read: 'The

mammoth task of shifting the thinking of the Northern Irish people from the violent tribal patterns of the past into new peace
making channels gets a great lift this fortnight, with direct access
to the resources of the Norwegian Peace Institute on the one
hand, and the potentially influential international conference in
Derry featuring such renowned peacemakers as Dom Helder
Camara'. In smaller type McKeown explained that he had received
from the Norwegian Institute a £4,500 scholarship usually reserved 'to eccentric native geniuses who don't fit into any of the normal categories'. and an invitation to a Pax Christi conference in
Derry.

On 9 June, a delegation came from the rank and file to the
Lisburn Road, to ask for a greater say in management.

'Peter McLachlan, came into an Executive meeting that night
and said that a delegation outside wanted to talk with us', said
Margaret Watson. 'They were allowed, and I mean allowed, in for
ten minutes. It was humiliating. They said they felt they weren't
in touch, that decisions were being taken by the Executive that
they only hear about much later and that something should be
done about it. It was pitiful. They couldn't put their finger on any
hard evidence but I knew what they meant. Suddenly I heard
Ciaran say their views would be taken into consideration, but
there was an agenda to be dealt with and he told them to leave. So
they went, like peasants who had just visited the tribal chiefs. At
the end of the meeting that night I asked Ciaran what was to be
done about the delegation. He said we had no more time to talk
about it but he looked around the room and appointed three people to look into it, telling them to visit the groups and report back
to the Executive'.

Next day she was in the supermarket, pushing a trolley and she
ran into another female member of the Executive, which then
comprised six women and three men.

'We started talking, little things you know about the movement
and that, and – I'll never forget it, – I was holding a cereal packet
when something the other woman said indicated to me that she
was feeling a bit uneasy too. Suddenly we both started to talk; it
was like opening a flood-gate and we discovered that there were
lots of little things we didn't feel great about and we both went
home and started telephoning other members'.

As a result, the ad hoc executive decided to hold a secret caucus that weekend when the three peace leaders, Williams, Corrigan and McKeown were out of the country. 'We met and talked, in the headquarters of the Ballynafeigh Peace Group. There was nothing sinister in it, and nothing sinister in our complaints, it was just that we all agreed that we were holding back at Executive meetings, letting the three of them make all the decisions. It was partly that we weren't used to politics ourselves, didn't know how to pass motions and so on, and partly that we couldn't believe that ordinary people like us could possibly have anything to offer. Whereas Betty and Mairead and Ciaran were lionized by the world and we were in awe of them. And you know, when the three of them were together, there was a special relationship between them, they had something between them that the rest of us couldn't touch'.

There was one dissenting voice at the caucus, she said, that of Steve McBride.

On the following Tuesday, Betty Williams arrived back from America and went to the Peace House. 'When I got in that evening, I heard roaring and shouting; you'd have thought the place was coming down. I asked what was happening and I was told that Betty was fighting with Peter McLachlan. He had told her about our meeting that weekend and what we had decided.

'Poor Peter, he went in to see Betty, all democratic, so that she and the other two would know we weren't doing anything behind their backs and she tore strips off him. They were together about an hour, and then Peter came out of the Board Room, white as a sheet and shaking. He was actually frightened. He told me he had never been spoken to like that in his life and he went home. I telephoned him that Tuesday night and he said he wasn't coming to the Executive meeting, and I told him he would have to; that if we didn't show and put on a united front that we could never complain again about not having control. So we went along and it was a quiet meeting, you'd think nothing had occured and it all went peacefully. As the meeting ended, I asked what was going to be done about the delegation we had received the previous week, and I was dismissed out of hand. I was shocked to see the way they were treating the complaints of the delegation and I went home that night very worried. I was sick over it, and I sat up most of the night thinking and I decided to resign. So I wrote a letter to Ciaran, left it in the Peace House next day, Friday, and the next night, Saturday, about midnight there came a knock on my door. Ciaran was there. He came in, talked to me, for several hours, and said I would be a big loss to the movement and that my complaints were valid.

'Then he did such a clever thing. He took out my letter and said, "this only says the words 'I wish to resign'. That is not the same thing as saying that you do resign. It isn't really a letter of resignation, if you look at it like that. It could be interpreted as merely a wish, unless things are straightened out". He then offered me a job I really liked. He said the Peace Movement should consider dismantling some part of the barricades that the Army called the peace line, the walls that sealed off Catholic from Protestants living in the same street and asked me to investigate the possibility of it in one specific area.

'I thought it was a great idea. If we could get Protestants and Catholics, living in the same street, to dismantle the wall that divided them, then we could show that there was hope that we could live together, without fear of each other. It would be a first step towards demilitarization'.

McKeown did not then or ever show the letter of resignation to the rest of the Executive. When I questioned him about this, he said that the Executive was an ad hoc one and as such was not bound by the formal rules that obtained after the October assembly, some months later.

Margaret Watson studied the designated areas for two weeks and made her report to the Executive. 'I was really excited. I told them that I had discovered it was possible to take down the barricades, that the people on both sides were willing to do so, but that it would take time. We would have to spend two years, first I said, dismantling the barricades in their minds. When I said that, Betty started to thump the table and she shouted at me that this was no pussyfooting peace movement, like Women Together or PACE, that we should act at once and that she personally would go to the area and start dismantling the wall brick by brick to set an example. I disagreed and she said that if we held back now, she would resign. I said there was no need for her to do that and I left the meeting. When we were outside I looked at Ciaran and told him to put my letter of resignation into effect immediately and I went home.

'Some nights later, after midnight, he knocked at my front door again, came in and asked me to reconsider. I told him my mind was made up. He said that they were about to have a peace rally on the Boyne and that an American was attending it, who was bringing over funds to distribute among the peace groups in Ireland. If there was a public split in the peace movement now, he said, they might not get the money. The rally was for the 2 July and I was about to go on holiday. I said I wouldn't withdraw my resignation but that I would keep quiet about it.

'What else could I do? I didn't want to be the first to split the movement. That seemed like an awful burden – it would have been sacreligious to cause dissension in a movement that everybody was calling the great hope for peace in Northern Ireland. Lots of people resigned over the next few months, quietly, like myself; nobody wanted the moral blame for desertion or destruction, or at least that's how it appeared to us. So members and even groups drifted quietly away, like snow off a ditch'.

When she returned from holiday, in August, Watson received a letter containing the minutes of two Executive meetings that had been held in July. 'My name was there, under apologies for not attending. They still didn't even know themselves that I had resigned. I wrote to them at once, saying I'd resigned at the end of June and wished the minutes to be amended accordingly. Ciaran read it out, as Chairman, and said "I wish she'd told me she had resigned".'

When I questioned McKeown about this, he said that Margaret Watson had resigned verbally so often that her words couldn't be taken seriously unless written down. The one written letter he had personally received was not valid since she had agreed that the words did not constitute a real resignation.

'I've often wondered since if McKeown steered us onto the Executive because we were political innocents', Watson said to me. 'He should try and handle me now. I've enrolled in Queen's University for a degree in political studies'.

In October, 1977 the movement had its first formal gathering in the prestigious Belfast Europa Hotel. McKeown introduced the theme of community politics suggesting that the Assembly of the Peace People legitimately regards itself as a model for community government of Northern Ireland. His motion was passed, after heated debate, though *Peace by Peace* recorded that 'many delegates felt restricted by their unfamiliarity with debate procedures and public speaking'.

Reality was introduced when the Relatives Action Committee came along and made an impassioned plea on behalf of the prisoners of H-Block, who were then still confining themselves to a blanket protest only. There was suspicion and unease during the three day assembly as the hard reality of H-Block contrasted crudely with the vision of governing Northern Ireland, and the rank and file were frankly bewildered. The gathering ended on 9 October.

On 10 October, Mairead and Betty were awarded the Nobel Peace Prize. A rush of mesmeric international publicity revived sagging morale and killed it within weeks as the women announced that they were keeping the money for themselves. The Executive under McKeown endorsed their decision. Disillusionment reached the point where only fifteen hundred people turned out to greet them in the cold December streets, after their return from Oslo to Belfast. City Hall delivered a cruel blow in its refusal to grant them a civic reception, as the politicians had their revenge on a movement leadership which had consistently humiliated them in public speeches. So removed at this stage were the Executive from the rank and file that they renamed the headquarters Fredheim, Norwegian for Peace House, and letters were signed Shalom. By Christmas 1977 they weren't even speaking English.

In January 1978 McKeown announced to the press that he was looking for a candidate for the European elections who was above the sectarian squabble. An Executive statement followed, confirming that the movement was now looking for means to ensure this, and the rank and file became even more confused about the distinction between vetting candidates and not being involved in party politics.

In February 1978, after a UDR man and child were killed by the Provos, the Peace People organised a peace train from the North to the Dublin headquarters of Provisional Sinn Fein. They arrived on Saturday as news broke that thirteen people had died the night before when the Provos fire-bombed the La Mons restaurant. The Peace picket attracted a pitiful few hundred supporters. McKeown, Corrigan and Williams called on families to inform on each other if any relative were engaged in violence. Betty said that Jack Lynch's suggestion, made some time before, of a future amnesty for political prisoners, gave the green light to the IRA.

Southern support melted away in the face of her faux pas. Northerners reeled, aghast, at the idea of informing.

The trio announced in April that they would not stand for re-election in the October assembly. McKeown relinquished chairmanship of the dwindling Trust Fund to James Galway, an elderly man who had seen the Wall Street Crash. The movement issued a trilogy of pamphlets by Galway on international banking and monetary policies, one of which was written in 1939, and was now published for the first time.

Support continued to erode, through apathy, confusion and misdirection, as Executive claims and proposed actions created an ever widening gulf between Fredheim and the peace groups that now met in each other's homes. The leadership suggested accompanying the British Army on all searches of all houses and to all interrogation centres in the north, though the Army processed 1,500 people per year through Castlereagh alone and the movement claimed only 1,000 members.

In October 1978 Peter McLachlan was elected Chairman of a dissipated Peace People, which proceeded to fade from the public view. McKeown, no longer on the Executive, continued to make headlines from the sidelines, arguing that the movement should become more involved in issues of justice. He campaigned vigorously for the dismantling of emergency legislation and special status for H-Block prisoners. The difference between special status and the political status claimed by the IRA eluded many of the rank and file who bitterly opposed the Provos.

McKeown then published in 1979 the *Path of Peace*, developing the theme of community politics that had severely disrupted the movement. He envisioned the creation in Northern Ireland of 'the most advanced democracy in the world', through the coming together, in an Assembly, of groups drawn from cantons of not more than 5,000 adults each. An Upper House or Senate would be composed of 'sporting, cultural and other networks'. By 1984, he wrote, there should be community policing, demilitarization, no emergency laws and community government.

'My certainty as I write these lines was not easily won', he wrote, but 'I started life with a bright little brain which was subsequently polished by a considerable amount of thinking and playing with ideas as a science and philosophy student of some ability .

. . it cannot hurt you to come with me for this hour' (of reading the pamphlet).

In August 1979, in *Peace by Peace*, McKeown reviewed his work over the last ten years and concluded 'Sometimes I wish that people who are not happy with the gift of life would hide themselves away and do the honourable thing – well I don't really but you know what I mean, all this belly-aching instead of rejoicing that they are alive and can breathe and feel the coolness of rain that grows the food they eat'. Anne Maguire was six months away from suicide.

In October 1979, the trio announced that they were standing for election because, Mairead told me 'the movement was going slow and we wanted to lift it back up a bit'. McKeown and Corrigan had their doubts about Betty, of course, expressed when McKeown told the outgoing Executive about her 'private life', but it was still necessary to provide a united front to a membership that was deeply troubled. McLachlan too, had his reservations about Betty, and he let it be known that he was embarrassed by the enthusiastically exaggerated claims she made to German business people about the attractive industrial packages available to investors in Northern Ireland. They were both working Trade Fairs in Germany and Peter had to deflate the rush of investors who came straight to him, from front woman Betty, for details.

The four stood successfully for re-election and Betty took a back seat on the Executive. The German trust issue was beginning to surface, as Betty continued to battle in Germany for funds. To which campaigns would the money be available? Ciaran's injustice, or Peter's projects? On one occasion Corrigan contributed to the Executive by saying 'I will really have to tell you more about Betty's moral character'.

On the night of 7 February, 1980, matters came to a head. A dispirited Williams resigned on the spot. McLachlan fought on and was asked to resign. Corrigan was elected Chairwoman to replace him. Resignations from branches and individuals flooded in. The spring Assembly of what remains of the movement took place in a priory in the countryside before thirty delegates. Corrigan announced that the movement would be taking the emphasis from politics to spiritual commitment. McKeown announced that he had resigned as editor of *Peace by Peace*, handing over to McBride. He was relinquishing all leadership functions this year, he told me, so that he could write a book on world peace that would synthesize European and Eastern thought, up to and including Camus.

'I should have no difficulty getting an outside publisher now'. he said.

It was all a far cry from the October 1977 issue of *Peace by Peace* when a massive front page photo of Betty and Mairead bore the thick large legend 'these rightly applauded ones who receive "the highest honour any human being can receive on this earth".' In a signed inside editorial McKeown wrote 'It is right that Betty and Mairead should, in a very personal way tremble before it (the Nobel award) because of the awesome responsibility it places on them for life. Everywhere they go and everything they say, from now until the day they die, will be reported as "Nobel Prizewinner Betty Williams said today" . . . or "Nobel Peace Prizewinner Mairead Corrigan today flew to . . ." If we fail to grasp the opportunity we will have deeply depressed a world that dared to hope; and for good measure we will have nailed Betty and Mairead to a cross of wasted suffering'.

Magill, August 1980.

Mairead Corrigan married Jackie Maguire, husband of her late sister Anne.

Betty Williams married an American businessman, and lives in America.

Death on the Border

The young British soldier guarding the border checkpoint between Co. Leitrim and Co. Fermanagh stood in the dark under a
makeshift signpost. The arrow-shaped boards nailed to a telegraph
pole indicated the distance from Manchester, London, Germany,
Cyprus, and points far, far away.

He did not know, nor did his companions in their concrete for-
tress know, how to get to Lisnaskea, a mere twenty miles ahead.
He had never heard of the Graham family, who live down a
laneway, off the main road, in the countryside that surrounds
Lisnaskea. Three Graham brothers, all part-time members of the
Ulster Defence Regiment, have been killed by the IRA since 1981.
Jimmy Graham, a school bus-driver, was shot dead on Friday, 1
February 1985, at Derrylin, not far in time or distance from where
the British soldiers now proclaimed themselves utterly lost.

'I haven't a clue why men join the UDR,' says the Church of
Ireland Rector Rev. Joshua McCloughlin, who buried Jimmy
Graham. The sermon he delivered to the thousands who came to
mourn, standing in the open on a wintry day because there was
no room for them in a small hilltop church that normally accom-
modates less than two hundred people, contained a warning that
no words of vilification would be unleashed upon the perceived
enemy. The rector reserved his scorn, instead, for the civil service,
those 'white-collared workers in London and Dublin,' making
their plans on 'ever shifting sands,' for the future of Ulster.

The rector vaguely disapproves of the whole notion of a locally
recruited UDR. 'They're being set up. They're soft targets.' He indicated softly that the gun corrupts, power corrupts, and that
neighbours who patrol neighbours run a very slight risk of corrup-
tion and a very grave danger of retribution.

In his sermon he had said 'I'm sure members of the UDR
recognise only too well that they are not above the law.' The regiment has come under mounting criticism across the North as a
sectarian force, whose members engage in off-duty killing with
legally-held guns. No such criticism, however, was voiced of the
Graham brothers by those Catholics living around Lisnaskea with
whom this reporter spoke. They were very much seen as members
of the community who were killed just because they were in the

UDR. Over and over again, the words were repeated 'It wasn't because they were Protestants. If they hadn't been in the UDR, they'd be alive today'.

Rev. Joshua McCloughlin points to the irony of that reasoning. It was precisely because they were Protestants, who felt under siege and unwanted that the Grahams uprooted from Monaghan in the post-Treaty twenties, and moved across the border into Fermanagh.

Their small family farm at Corrard, near Lisnaskea could not support all the brothers and sisters, and Albert Graham, when his time came, moved out and into a nearby railway cottage to start a family of his own. He reared five sons and two daughters in that little house, on a small patch of land at the foothills, working as a labourer, supplementing both his income and social life as a member of the 'B Specials'. His children in turn moved out to marry, working mainly in unskilled poorly paid jobs. Wherever they went, though, they erected the family crest, two eagles, one on each of the gateposts that guarded the pathway to their homes.

When the British Army arrived and the B Specials were disbanded, and replaced in April 1970 by the Ulster Defence Regiment, Mr Graham joined up, along with three of his sons, Jimmy, Ronnie and Cecil, and a daughter, Hilary. Fermanagh, which shares the North's longest border with the South, was becoming increasingly militarised. A voting population of 63,000 is today patrolled by 2,318 security personnel, a ratio of one legally armed person to twenty-eight civilian adults, half of whom are politically, at least, disaffected nationalists who once made Belfast prisoner Bobby Sands their MP. It is recognised by all sides that the IRA incursors are imported from outside Fermanagh.

The Graham family came through the seventies relatively unscathed, though Hilary was hospitalised for several months after being knocked down by a car which crashed through a security checkpoint. She has since died from cancer. The UDR, comprising 260 full-time members, and 360 part-timers, lost twelve members in that decade, six of whom were shot dead in 1972, the year of Bloody Sunday.

In 1981, the year of the hunger strikes when the security and republic profile of the north became more deeply etched, three part-time members of the UDR were killed in Fermanagh. The first to die was Ronnie Graham, a 38-year-old married man with two children. On a Friday morning in June he drove his children to school, dropped his wife off at his sister's house, and started his lorry round, delivering coal, milk and groceries to outlying homesteads in the bleakly beautiful moorland that surrounds Lough Erne. He was ambushed at a farmhouse door, on the road to Derrylin, within sight of the portacabin where his younger brother Norman lived.

At his funeral, attended by thousands, where a piper played the lament, the rector said 'In the normal course of events, his name would not make the headlines . . . this family will not be ordinary again.'

Five months later his brother Cecil was shot dead. Cecil Graham had married a local Catholic, Mary Rice, who worked alongside him in the cotton factory at Lisnaskea, and they set up home in a portacabin. His elderly uncle, a bachelor who inherited the original family farm at Corrard, came to live alongside them in another portacabin, and Cecil worked the holding in his spare time, with a herd of sixteen cattle. When the uncle died, leaving him the ancestral farm, Cecil Graham began to build a bungalow on the land, financing the enterprise with the couple's factory earnings, and his part-time UDR work.

Mary, who had finally become pregnant after nine years, due to having only one ovary, left the factory when a twelve-hour shift was introduced. 'That left us short of money. Cecil would sell off a beast to buy bricks, finish his shift and go down to build the house, and put in nights and weekends with the UDR.' The current minimum pay is £16 per eight-hour tour of duty.

They had barely moved into their new home when the baby was born prematurely, with a murmur in the heart. With her husband out patrolling at night, and the infant ailing. Mary could get little sleep so she moved back into her parent's home until the health of mother and child should be restored.

Her parents lived in Donagh, a village that has been described as the only real ghetto in the county. All forty-nine families there are Catholic. Donagh, in November 1981, was still hung with black flags of mourning for the hunger strikers. On the night of 7 November, Cecil Graham went to visit his wife and five-week-old son. He stayed for an hour, left after 11pm and was shot while getting into his car.

Mary's father, who had served as a boy soldier with the British Army at Dunkirk in 1945, heard the gunfire, switched off the lights, and ordered his family to stay in their bedrooms. He opened the door, peered out into the street, and 'saw a hand come up by the wheel of the car. Then Cecil pulled himself backwards up the path, and I brought him into the hall. His mouth and stomach were shot to pieces.' The village remained in darkness.

Cecil Graham died in a Belfast hospital two days later. Despite his hard working life, and though he did finally finish the bungalow, he left a bank overdraft of £5,000. Mary leased the bungalow and farm, her parents left Donagh, and the two families now live side by side in a Council estate in Lisnaskea. Though she married Cecil Graham in the Church of Ireland, and her son was baptised into that faith, she will now rear him as a Catholic, she says. 'Religion doesn't matter, and politics don't matter either, but I'm back with my family and I don't want him to grow up different to his cousins.'

She does not see herself returning to the farm. 'People might point and say look at how I got it.' She maintains contact with the Graham family through one of the two surviving brothers, Kenneth, who is engaged to her sister. 'He met her long before I met Cecil.'

The death of Cecil Graham was overshadowed and overtaken by that of Unionist Assembly member Rev. Robert Bradford who was assassinated a few days later in Belfast. Even as the loyalist workers of Fermanagh joined in a province-wide work stoppage in protest at the assassination, a married neighbour of the Grahams, Albert Beacom, also a part-time UDR member, was shot dead in the farmyard of his home.

That was the week also when the Rev Ivan Foster, DUP Assembly member for Fermanagh, announced the formation in the country of a 'Third Force' which would voluntarily and without legal constraints, supplement the work of the RUC, UDR and British Army. Masked men were paraded through the streets of Enniskillen.

With Albert Graham retired, and two sons and a daughter dead, Jimmy Graham was the only one of the family still in the service of the UDR. A married man with two children, he worked as a school caretaker cum school bus driver, supplementing his wages with a quite substantial income as a part-time officer of the UDR.

His wife Lily also had a part-time job in the Lisnaskea High School.

The small cottage in which they lived was renovated into a smart two-storey farmhouse with outhouses in which pigs were reared. Jimmy Graham managed to buy four acres which he hoped to use for horse breeding. Acknowledged locally as what the minister who buried him called 'a self-willed man', Jimmy Graham took his military duty as seriously as he took his civilian work.

He had spent three years in the Territorial Army before joining the UDR in 1970, and his service to Queen and country was recognised in January 1985, when he was awarded the British Empire Medal. Long before his brothers were shot dead, Mr. Graham had twice escaped ambush, once as he came out of his home, and once when a bullet grazed his shoulder as he drove the school bus.

On the first day of February 1985, as he waited in his bus outside a Catholic primary school in Derrylin, ready to drive children to the swimming pool in Enniskillen, the IRA killed him He did not have time, the local newspaper reported, to draw the service pistol which off-duty members are allowed to carry at all times. He died a few miles from where his brother Ronnie was killed.

His wife Lily heard the news later that morning as she went shopping in Lisnaskea. She knew, she said, that there was something wrong when she went into the drapery store. Everybody was standing there, shocked, and staring at her. The Church of Ireland Bishop of his diocese flew back from New York for the funeral.

The news of Jimmy's death was too much for Ronnie Graham's widow, Josie. Just two weeks before that a 21-year-old part-time member of the UDR had come courting her daughter. As he left the house, a hail of bullets struck him. Although he survived, Josie Graham did not survive the sight of him 'crawling back up the path to the door,' in the words of her daughter. Josie moved her family out of the countryside and into a council house in Maguiresbridge, and she was brought to a mental home in Omagh, suffering from a nervous breakdown. She is allowed to return home at weekends.

Mary Graham attends a psychiatrist every fortnight.

Lily Graham refuses to speak to reporters from Dublin, saying 'The South harbours the IRA'.

Lily Graham did say to her local newspaper that though she had lived in fear, night after night, for Jimmy's life, she had nothing but praise for her Catholic neighbours. They would have come to the wake, but for fear of the IRA. One of those Catholic neighbours told *Magill* that he did not dare go to Lily's house for fear of 'Jimmy's friends. And the embarrassment of it. What could I say, when I knew Jimmy would not have been killed, but for being in the UDR.' He went to the cemetery and was lost among the thousands who thronged it.

Ken Maginnis, Westminster Unionist MP for the area and former UDR man cum teacher has called for increased security forces in Fermanagh. A member of the House of Commons Select Committee for Defence, he was one of two MPs who recently volunteered to fly to Norway to observe the British Army and Navy engage in the exercise 'Cold Winter'. The other volunteer for the thankless courtesy task was a newly by-elected Tory MP. The temperature in the snow-bound wilds of Norway was thirty degrees below zero. 'There is no doubt about our Britishness,' said Maginnis on the exercise. 'These are the reasons why I was invited.'

Back in Fermanagh, Kenny Graham lives still with his father in the railway cottage, and works with a brother-in-law, mending old cars. He refuses to talk to journalists and will not allow his father to be interviewed. He never did join the UDR.

Nor did his only surviving brother Norman. Norman, who works in a Lisnaskea factory, married a local Catholic, with whom he now lives in a portacabin, set on concrete blocks, alongside the small corrugatged iron house in which his wife Pam and her eleven brothers and sisters were reared. Pam's bachelor brother is the sole occupant of the little house, the others having gone to England. The six children of Co. Fermanagh's retiring Chief of Police are also, incidentally, living and working in England.

Norman, Pam, their infant daughter, and Pam's brother share a small patch of land on which they grow vegetables, raise pet rabbits, and train hunting dogs. Occasionally, duck and pheasant are bagged. The place is bright and neat as a poor and honourable pin. Two eagles on pillar post. guard them. Away up in the graveyard, on the graves of Ronnie and Jimmy, who lie back to back beneath a tombstone that says 'Murdered by the IRA', a withered wreath bears the inscription, 'The day thou gavest, Lord, is ended.'

Angela Whoriskey

The supergrass system in the North effectively ended last month when the RUC announced that their informer, Angela Whoriskey from Derry, would not testify. The news has been passed off by the establishment here and in Britain as a victory for the Anglo-Irish agreement. It is evidence, the suggestion goes, of reform of the legal system, and Northern nationalists should take comfort from this.

Nonsense.

The supergrass system collapsed under the weight of its own filth. The single, most sustained, perversion of law and social mores the North has ever seen ended when the RUC finally pushed a member of the weakest section of the community too far. They drove Angela Whoriskey mad. She is literally insane.

Angela Whoriskey was a prime supergrass target. She was socially vulnerable, of low intelligence, wandering adrift in her own home-town of Derry. A short stay in a pyschiatric hospital was followed by pregnancy and homelessness. She was unmarried. She was dependent on the charity of acquaintances. Shortly after the birth of her baby, the RUC swooped on her, brought her to Castlereagh interrogation centre, separated her from her child, who was taken to a place unknown, and questioned her for seven days. Her father and brothers were swept from the city, courtesy of the RUC, and sent abroad.

In those circumstances, and under that pressure, she agreed with everything they wanted to know, including, clearly, things she didn't know herself, since charges levelled in consequence against twenty Derry people have now been withdrawn.

Those against whom she pointed the finger, and whom she identified when she met them in their cells, thought at the time that she had been subjected to mind-bending drugs, such was her demented demeanour. She had not. She had merely been subjected to the RUC, as later reports showed.

Those reports came from women in Armagh jail, and subsequently in Maghaberry prison, to which the Armagh prisoners had been transferred. People who never knew Angela Whoriskey, and who shared a prison block with her, sent word out that she was a pitiful, deranged figure, wandering the corridor and mumbling and crying out.

She was kept in that condition, in prison, for the last eighteen months, while the supergrass charges moved ponderously through the courts. This enabled the RUC to keep some of those whom she charged in prison, without bail. This is the phenomenon known as internment by remand.

All of those accused by her were set free last month. They were not even allowed into court to hear the charges dropped. They were forced to remain in the foyer of Derry courthouse, while their fate was decided inside, out of their view and hearing, in a classic demonstration of Northern justice.

Angela Whoriskey remains in jail. It was part of the supergrass deal that she plead guilty herself, to a charge of murder, with the understanding that her long sentence would be commuted upon successful conclusion of the supergrass case. The fate of this lonely, isolated, maddened woman, and her baby – whereabouts unknown – is a subject of speculation. She is, Christ help her, at the mercy of the RUC and the British Home Office. No Irish authority has made representations on her behalf.

This is supposed to be a victory for the Anglo-Irish agreement, and a comfort to nationalists, and a source of joy to the people of Derry. It is no such thing.

In Dublin, 3 November 1986.

The Class of '68

Some school-children remain in your mind, years after you taught them, and you wonder whatever became of them. It is particularly difficult to trace girls, since most of them get married and give up their original surnames.

For a long time now I have been curious about a group of teenage females who were placed in my charge, in Derry, in 1968, when I was given a three month substitute teaching job.

It was made clear to me that if I could keep them quiet, I would have achieved a great deal. They belonged to a difficult class, and showed not the remotest interest in learning. With only one year of school left, they had but one thought in mind – getting a job.

That being so, I concentrated a lot of effort into reducing them to a state of happy physical exhaustion. While other girls swotted over reading, writing and arithmetic, my lot were out on the playing field, where they engaged in everything from football to American baseball. Once in a while, I took them on a tour of Creggan Estate, where the school was situated, and got them to write down the names of the streets where most of them lived. It was a desperate attempt to encourage them towards writing and spelling.

After a month of touring the estate, they progressed to writing out the words of rock and roll songs. The Beatles were popular, and there used to be dead silence in class while they listened to the records I played, and tried to record the lyrics.

When things got really desperate, which was usually once a day, I relied on the most untried method of all – I used to march them down the hill towards my mother's house, bring them in, and give them tea and biscuits.

In her presence, they were all well behaved as one would expect any Derry girl to be. Mothers command a respect that teachers do not.

One girl, whose mother was dead, took to hanging around our house after school closed. My mother would call her in from the street and chat with her. Years later, I met the girl's father and was impressed. He was a Republican of the old school, and heavily engaged in the fight for civil rights. Then I lost touch.

Now I know what happened to her in the interim.

A young Republican man, himself an orphan, came to lodge in her father's house. She started to date him, and became pregnant by him.

He was as young and cheerful and feckless as herself. She became pregnant. On his way to the wedding, he stopped off with the best man and bought a bottle of vodka, and had a couple of drinks. The bottle, in the paper, shows in their wedding picture.

He joined the INLA.

Their marriage deteriorated, and blows were struck, by both sides. She had two babies and he ended up in jail, serving a long sentence.

She started a relationship with another man. Her husband sued for a divorce.

Then the hunger strike of 1981 started.

The young man volunteered.

He forbade his wife to visit him in hospital.

As he lay dying, his children were brought to him. Blind by now, he could only feel the outline of their young bodies.

His wife was informed that he would not be buried, if he died, from her home, and that she would not be allowed to attend his funeral.

He was buried from his sister's house, the children followed his hearse, and his wife remained invisible.

She has since had three children by the man whom she met while her husband was in prison, but she refused to marry him and all five children now carry the hunger-striker's surname. She spends long periods in a mental home. The history of these and other pupils of the class of '68 is contained in a devastatingly sad book about the hunger strike, called *Ten men dead*, by David Beresford.

Kerry's Eye 6-11 August 1987.

Nuclear War

Operation Lionheart and Nuclear War

In the last fortnight of this month NATO soldiers will pretend to live out the last days of the world. World War Three, or 'Operation Lionheart' to use their macho code, will be stage-managed in West Germany from September 15 to September 30, complete with hurriedly-dug mass graves, computerised bombing and sound and fury signalling, they say, nothing.

It will be a mock war, of course. Militarists are much given to mocking, as was President Reagan when he announced during a radio sound test that the bombing of Russia would commence in five minutes.

The inclination to smile has lessened on two real occasions in the recent past. There was that heart-stopping moment when moral majority leader, Billy Graham, claimed to have discussed the possibility of nuclear holocaust with Mr. Reagan. The President, he said, agreed that it might take place son.

Then there was the revelation in the *New Statesman* that Margaret Thatcher had made contingency plans to wipe out a city in Argentina with a nuclear missile – just like that – should the Falklands war go against her.

This last revelation occasioned no outcry whatsoever.

Why was that, do you think?

It could be that we have forgotten already the 40th anniversary, so recently commemorated, of the wiping out of the people and city of Hiroshima. That particular atomic bombing put a quick halt to the Japanese gallop, but the point of the commemoration was to swear publicly 'never again', or at least not like that.

Trust us, the bureaucrats, technologists, and militarists, are saying. If you don't trust them, or feel that the burden of decision-making about the future of the world should be shared among more than the few, you should head for Greenham Common on September 10.

Irish Women for Disarmament will be leaving Dublin on that day by boat, to spend ten days with their sisters over there, and they can be contacted through Chris Mulvey at Dublin 724632.

These are the women, you might remember who posed such a

threat to President Reagan and his nuclear policy that the gardai arrested them in the Phoenix Park while the President was drinking beer in Ballyporeen, and held them under no known law in the Bridewell for 36 hours.

They are now suing the guards.

They would prefer not to have to sue Reagan or Thatcher for behaviour that could lead to a breach of the very world. They would prefer to avoid nuclear holocausts and wonder if you have any ideas on the subject.

Whether you agree or not, support the NATO mock war or not, these women would like to hear from you or about you for ten seconds, or ten minutes, or ten days, during the ten days they will be spending at Greenham.

All they ask of us is that we speak for ourselves, and take seriously a mock war that Ronald Reagan and Margaret Thatcher have clearly intimated might be no joke at all.

Irish Press, 6 September 1984.

Chernobyl

I used to wonder what I really would do when the news came that I had not much longer to live. Generally, I felt that I'd be too sick in bed to give a damn, or too old and frail to book a night out on the town in New York. I wondered if I'd feel bitter about having paid into a pension fund for decades, with only weeks left to spend it. Naturally, I flattered myself that I'd ring up my nearest and dearest, passing on noble wishes that they'd be happy, nevertheless, without me, and recalling their many acts of love and kindness to me.

It wasn't a bit like that in London, last week, when the evening papers screamed that 2,000 people were dead in Russia, the lethal cloud was on its way to Europe, and anyone living within one hundred miles of a nuclear reactor was living on borrowed time. Standing outside a tube station on the Holloway Road, I read the paper and did what everybody else did – got on with normal life.

Try as I might, over a lovely greasy breakfast in a London cafe, to put my affairs in order, and plan a few really sensational events for the short number of years remaining to me, I could come up with nothing spectacular or noble. I didn't even bother to ring home.

Towards midnight, however – they say it takes a while for shock to set in – I swung into action. I could have supper in the fish and chipper, or I could dine in a newly opened Indian fish restaurant, where the grilled spiced prawns were fetching rave reviews. The difference in price between the two places was a small fortune.

Standing at the counter of the fish and chipper, I heard Pete Murray interrupt his late night music and chat radio show to say that the expert on nuclear disaster had arrived in his studio and would be answering questions until 2 a.m.

I had not heard such sombre tones since the Northern Ireland branch of the BBC did an hourly summary on the run-down of the power stations during the Ulster Workers' Strike in 1974. Soon, soon, the commentators said then, there'd be no more hot water; we were passing the point of no return and the sewers would be flooding the streets, and we'd be years waiting for the electricity to get turned on again.

Everybody in Derry believed these guys, and my mother kept the immersion switched on all week, and we were all forced to have two baths daily so as not to waste the boiling flow. Months later, when the strike was over and the power stations worked merrily away, the electricity bill came in.

It was enormous.

My mother didn't regret a penny of it.

That week, she said, was the first, last and only time in her life when she didn't give a damn about money, said to hell with poverty, and blow the expense. She would bear the memory of such luxury for the rest of her life.

So I cancelled my order of ray and chips, turned on my heel in the London cafe, and went next door to the Indian restaurant. The more the expert lamented the disaster and predicted more — for all the waiters were listening to the radio — the more I ordered. I had the advantage of not paying in cash. Using a plastic card, I figured the bill would not arrive for at least a month, by which time the world's finances would be in chaos? American Express would surely have vacated their headquarters in nuclear-stations dotted Europe, and moved to Kerry, and by the time they'd sorted things out, we'd all be dying anyway and Justice Kevin Lynch himself would hardly be still holding court, demanding that I account for the errors of my ways.

So I spent, spent, spent for three days in London. The initial shock is now over of course, and people are reassuring themselves that it couldn't happen here, not in Europe, certainly not in England, and definitely not in Sellafield, within whose shadow we in Ireland live.

It also occurs to me that London restaurant owners were on to a good thing, playing the Pete Murray show loudly over their radios and luring the customers to part with their remaining few quid.

Nevertheless, I have not broken off the love affair with my plastic card. News does not necessarily travel fast, and radiation sickness assuredly does not. The fall-out from Chernobyl, in terms of information and those deadly particles, is not over yet by a long chalk. It could be that we are living in very dangerous times.

If we're going to go out with a bang, I intend to go out broke. I'll pay my phone bill, of course, and the mortgage and the TV licence, and attend to little matters like that. This is called caution.

So know I know . . . not with a bang, but a whimper, does a human being meet the end of the world. A couple of prawns, that's all I snatched from it.

A couple of lousy prawns.

Kerry's Eye, 1-7 May 1986.

The Women's Room

You can tell from the conversation in a sauna, the new women's room, how fares the world. For a while there we wondered what we'd talk about when we didn't have the Pope to kick around any more; in the post-christian, private Catholic, era after divorce, would words fail us?

This is how the conversation went last week.

If Sellafield melted down, she would get into her car, put her foot on the accelerator, and head for County Clare, said Mary. That would put about two hundred and fifty miles between her and the radiation. With a fair wind, hopefully in her face and blowing it all back to England, she could stay in the banner county until the all-clear came.

Martha argued that 250 miles was no protection at all. She had studied the map after Chernobyl, was now an expert on the Ukraine, had mentally transposed it onto Ireland, and come up with the conclusion that the whole of our island would come under the cloud from Sellafield. She, therefore, would proceed at her leisure to Donegal, there to die, but at least she'd die at home.

Maureen said she would go to Australia. Every woman in the sauna came up with an immediate reason why Maureen was talking rubbish. She'd have to catch a connecting flight from London, assuming she could get on the plane at Dublin, and the trains and planes from Kiev were booked up the minute they heard about nearby Chernobyl. London, in any case, would be radiated and the Aussies were hardly likely to want glowing immigrants arriving on their shores spreading disease.

The appalling truth spread like a cloud over Sellafield as we pondered the worst fate of all: everybody in Ireland would be quarantined, on this island, for the rest of our lives, and the lives of our children's lives, and the lives of the children of our children.

We wouldn't even be able to have abortions, murmured Mary.

They'd introduce abortion on the instructions of the Pope himself, snarled Martha.

We could head for Clare and catch a boat to America, Maureen was still hatching escape plans.

The American gun-boats, off-shore, would sink us, Mary said;

the Yanks don't want diseased immigrants either.

Maureen wondered if the grants for refurbishing houses could be revised to include the building of bunkers. Ten thousand quid would only get you a place that was safe for thirty days, said Martha, who had read the advertisement placed by the entrepreneurs within a week of Chernobyl exploding. After that you'd have to come out and radiate like everybody else.

If there was anybody else.

There would be the government lads down in Athlone, said Mary, who knows all about the government bunker, now that we have to pay attention to such details. We tried to envisage the emergency coalition government of Garret, Charlie, Dick and Dessie, coming out of the bunker in Athlone. The inanity of this precluded the most wan of smiles.

Maureen thought we all should go to Australia, right now, before Sellafield goes up. Where would we get the money? How would we acquire the visas? The petty constraints of life before radiation reduced us to gloom.

Martha thought that she had read somewhere, anyway, that Australia had nuclear reactors, just waiting like the rest of them to blow up; wasn't there something in the paper, years ago, about a woman's protest peace camp on the edge of Alice Springs, or was it Perth? She would check it out and report back to us; we'd all have to check things out and report back on exactly where the nuclear stations are located on the globe.

Can the stations be shut down; how long does it take to catch leukaemia; how does the central nervous system operate; how many centuries must pass before polluted soil is declared radiation free? These are the questions posed as part of normal conversation in the women's rooms, these days. Meantime, Archbishop Mac Namara wants us to stay married, for the rest of our lives, no matter how unhappy or brutal or lethal the relationship; no matter even if the man has long since left the house; and whether or no, and even if, the very air that we breathe together is poisoned.

In Dublin, 15 May 1986.

Unfinished
Business

Cavan Rape

The most extraordinary and disturbing feature of last week's rape case which is now the subject of two inquiries, is not that senior counsel prosecuting on behalf of the state was absent for most of the trial. It is the summing up of the trial made by Mr Justice Frank Roe, in his lengthy address to the jury, before they retired to ponder their verdict.

Judge Roe erred in one matter of fact; his presentation of another fact is arguable; and his attitude to the self-incriminating statement of the alleged rapist is remarkable.

These three matters were, he made it clear to the jury, inter-related. They were all to do with the amount of drink consumed by the accused, and the effects such drinking would have on any declaration subsequently made by him, to the gardai. In effect, the judge invited the jury to consider if the man's confession of rape was merely a drunken boasting fantasy, the commonplace details of which would feature in any drunkard's fantasy about a commonplace rape.

The error of fact occurred when Mr Justice Roe announced that the man had consumed, on the night of the rape, 'nine pints and a bottle of vodka'. At no time in the course of the trial did either prosecution or defence suggest that he had consumed this amount.

The man's statement referred to 'six pints and a naggin of vodka'. The accused himself denied in court that he had ever drunk vodka, pleading that he could not drink spirits of any kind because of an ulcer condition.

He also insisted that he was not drunk on the night in question. His father testified that he had arrived home sober. The raped woman did not suggest that her attacker was blind drunk, though she knew he had taken alcohol.

Judge Roe also invited the jury to consider the fact that the accused man had made his confession to the gardai a 'short time' after consuming the prodigious amount suggested. The time factor weighed heavily in the judge's summary. The confession was in fact made the day after the pubs had closed, during which time, the accused man told the court, he had gone home to bed, had a night's sleep and his breakfast. In the opinion of the judge, this fifteen hour break constituted a short interval.

In the judge's further opinion the amount of drink taken and the 'short' interval elapsing before the man made a statement, should be taken into account when considering the content of that statement. It was a true fact that the man had voluntarily made the statement but the judge asked, were the contents truthful?

In a curious analogy about night-life in Cavan, the judge invited the jury to consider what their attitude might be to people who made statements after 'leaving nightclubs in Dublin'. Such people might have come upon a traffic incident or a family row, he said, and given evidence to what they had seen or heard.

'Would it be safe to convict on evidence like that?' he asked. The accused had done a tour of Cavan pubs and then made a statement. (Would it be safe to convict on evidence like that?)

In theory, of course, a jury is free to accept or reject the opinion of a judge, given in trial summary. They must only be bound by a judge when that judge is directing them on matters of law. The opinion of the judge, prosecution and defence lawyers is not binding on them.

In this case, the jury spent less than fifteen minutes making up its own mind, after hearing the judge's considerably longer examination of his own.

The attitude of the judge to the woman who was raped and to her male friends, is also worthy of remark. She testified candidly in court to having had a boyfriend since her marriage ended four years ago. She also formed friendships with other men, and these friends visited her at home. Her boyfriend who also testified, confirmed their relationship, and the social nature of night life in Cavan – people go ceilidhing after the pubs close. On the night of the rape, he had gone to see the woman.

'The raped woman', said the judge, dealing with the case made by the defence, 'is a deserted wife . . . we must face the facts. It appears that it is not unusual for her boyfriend and perhaps other men to come to her home, quite late at night, sometimes after the public houses have closed'. He added that this did not mean that the woman was 'keeping a house of ill fame'.

He did not explain, in consequence, what facts he therefore wished the jury to face in considering her social life.

Why raise them, if the facts of the woman's social life were innocent of any ill fame whatever? Why not, indeed, dismiss them?

As regards the woman's boyfriend, the judge stressed that he was utterly and totally innocent of any implication whatever in the rape. He was not the rapist, nor was he alleged to be the rapist, a fact which also was stressed by the alleged rapist's lawyer. This man was, all sides agreed, the woman's boyfriend and nothing more nor less than that, on the night in question.

However, said the judge to the jury in reference to this innocent man and his socialising that night, 'you know what goes on, especially when the pubs have closed and people are anxious not to go home, anxious to go somewhere else. You know what happens. Are people who do these things reliable witnesses?'

He wanted the jury to consider the reliability of the witness borne by the innocent man, under oath, that he had called to the woman's house that night, knocked on the front and back doors, and gone away without receiving an answer.

The defence had insisted that this man had been inside the woman's house an hour before the rape, and a witness was called to that effect. In his summing up, Judge Roe left unresolved the question of whether the man had been knocking at the door or actually coming out of the house.

Since this man had not raped the woman, it might appear to matter not one whit whether he had been in her house or not – unless of course, he was reluctant to admit to having been with her before the rape occurred, and that the raped woman shared this reluctance. If they were both to lie about this, the jury would be entitled to conclude that they lied about other matters.

Except of course that the judge, the defence and the prosecution all stressed repeatedly that the woman and her boyfriend were telling two absolute truths about the night in question. The first truth was that the woman had been raped. The second truth was that she had not been raped by her boyfriend.

In face of that, the judge's suggestion that the jury 'face the facts' about their relationship and their activities is puzzling. Equally puzzling is the attitude of defence counsel Paddy McEntee to the woman's own boyfriend.

It was Mr McEntee himself who first assured the court that this man was a completely innocent party on the night in question. Having said that, Mr McEntee asked him why he had been 'sniffing' around her 'front and back doors' an hour before the rape occurred. Mr McEntee used the term 'sniffing' repeatedly, while he questioned this innocent man, and used it again in his final summary to the jury of the evidence they had heard.

The scenario painted by both him and the judge, of a man 'sniffing' around the home of a 'deserted wife', after the pubs 'have closed', and the innuendo that 'you know what goes on . . . you know what happens?' contrasted luridly with their solemn assurances to the jury that the man was also, of course, completely innocent of any wrongdoing, and that the raped woman was not keeping a house of ill fame.

Why create this atmosphere? What would it matter if every man in Ireland had been in her house in an atmosphere of tomcattery five minutes before the rape occurred? Previous sexual history does not alter the fact that when a woman says 'no' she means 'no'.

The current inquiries being properly conducted into the State's prosecution of this rape case are, of course, to be welcomed. The State's senior legal counsel was absent for most of the case, and certainly during crucial parts of it. Mr Paul Carney, the absent counsel admitted to *The Irish Press* that it was 'unusual' for a senior counsel not to sum up.

Whatever Mr Carney's explanation for this 'unusual' occurrence and for his decision to leave the prosecution of the case effectively in the hands of his junior counsel, if the term 'senior counsel' is to have any meaning in the ordinary sense of the word, the raped woman was clearly denied the superior experience of the best person for the job.

Her junior counsel, for instance, spent less than ten minutes summarising the State's case to the jury, while the accused man's senior counsel spent nearly two hours refuting the State's case in his final summing up.

To confine the public inquiries to this matter alone, however, is to suggest that the only disturbing feature of last week's rape trial was the absence of Mr Carney. In calling him to sole account, the Director of Public Prosecutions and the Bar Council are avoiding the more painful and urgent task of reviewing the climate and conduct of rape cases generally, by all sides. That climate stinks.

Irish Press, 4 June 1987.

Marital Rape

Anne O'Donnell, publicity director of the Rape Crisis Centre, is a joy. She is the happiest feminist in Ireland, and the very sight of her brings happiness to feminist souls. Her taste in earrings, punk hairstyle, and peacock clothes is legendary. It belies her rigid adherence to principles.

Her strongest principle is that on Tuesday nights, no one is allowed into her home except her husband and infant son, and they can only stay there provided they keep absolutely quiet between ten past ten and ten past eleven. During that hour, the phone is also taken off the hook. Anne O'Donnell watches *Dallas* on telly then. If an episode is particularly good, she will watch it again on BBC on Wednesday night. Hard though it is to admit, it is possible that she knows even move about *Dallas* than this correspondent.

It is a measure of her commitment to the Rape Crisis Centre, then, that she is prepared to give up one Tuesday night in the month of November to chair a public meeting. The meeting will address itself to a campaign, ending on 17 November, which the RCC is conducting countrywide. The centre wants the law reviewed to include marital rape as a crime. A man who rapes a woman is a rapist, even if he is her husband. The law does not recognise this principle. The law allows a woman to have her husband excluded from the marital home, if he breaks her jaw or smashes up the furniture. The police will, if necessary, intervene to keep such a man out of the house. However, if he should return, pin his wife to the bed, and rape her, the law will find him guilty merely of breaking the terms of the barring order and going into the house, against the judge's wish. What he does in bed, to his wife (or on the floor, or on the table), is none of the law's concern, provided he uses his penis.

A husband's penis is a legal instrument within the meaning of the marital contract. His bunched fist is not, and he can be jailed for using it. He can, however, use his penis at will. It is not just husbands debarred from the family home who rape their wives. Husbands who otherwise behave impeccably – hand up their wages, pat the children on the head, stay sober, come home every night after work – are also capable of raping their wives, and do so, on a scale sufficiently widespread to have alarmed the RCC which has to deal with the wife-victim.

The law's reluctance to recognise this fact stems from a concept of marriage that is patriarchal and religious. This concept holds that a man has conjugal rights. Put simply, it means that a man has the right to sexual intercourse with his wife, by virtue of marrying her, whether she wants the intercourse or not.

Indeed the Catholic Church goes further. If sexual intercourse does not take place, says the church, the marriage is invalid. It doesn't even matter that the man might not want sexual intercourse. The couple has to do what the church wants them to do, or the marriage is not theologically legal. A few years ago in England, the church refused a chapel wedding to a paraplegic soldier who wanted to marry the nurse who had cared for him during his illness. They were deeply in love. The couple knew that the soldier was incapable of having sexual intercourse, in the sense of the penis penetrating the vagina, but this didn't matter to them. There are other ways of having sexual pleasure. And even if they weren't interested in sexual pleasure, they were deeply interested in, and in love with, each other.

Nope, said the church.

Luckily for the human race, most men and women who marry each other want very much to have sexual intercourse. They see the marital contract as not so much a bind, but an absolute licence to have it off morning, noon and night, to the applause of grinning relatives and friends who shoo them off on their honeymoon, and plot their progress discreetly ever after, in the form of a silly question: 'Shall we soon hear the patter of tiny feet?' The patter of tiny feet is usually the last thing on the minds of the deliriously fornicating couple. For which, let us give praise. Sex can be smashing, and everybody should engage in it as often as they can. Providing there is mutual agreement. It doesn't always work, of course but there you are, the world is not perfect, and the law is sensible: you can't bring a partner to court for failure to please.

If you could, and we were honest, the courts would be packed with litigants.

Sex is ruinous, and criminal, where it is used as a weapon against another person. There is no need to dwell here on the vileness of rape, though rape is all that the Rape Crisis Centre is dwelling on, when it asks that no man, regardless of marital status, should be allowed to perpetrate sexual assault upon a woman. What man, in any case, would want to push himself in where he is not wanted?

Answer: a rapist, be he bishop, politician, pop singer, boy or husband.

The RCC wants rape criminalised, no matter what the relationship between the rapist and the victim. On Saturday, 1 November, the centre will be collecting signatures in support of this principle throughout the country. Marital rape is considered a crime in other lands. Once more, we are being offered a chance to join civilised society.

In Dublin, 30 October 1986.

Child Sexual Abuse

The sexual abuse of children, said District Justice Herbert Wine, had become all too prevalent in the last year or two. 'We read about it in the newspapers and hear about it on TV.'

He was wrong, of course. Child sexual abuse is not a new phenomenon. What is new is the public admission that it happens, and our attempts to cope with it. As with the revelations in the seventies of widespread wife-battery and rape, and reaction to those revelations – disbelief, ignorance, the first faltering attempts of underfunded voluntary agencies to cope, the establishment of official channels, the first surfacing in court, the fumbling reaction of the judiciary, and then the legal measures – so it is now with child abuse.

The case heard in Dun Laoghaire court last week and the manner in which the case was handled on all sides shows that officialdom needs to do more than just read about in newspapers and watch it on TV.

The people involved were instructed to appear in court at ten thirty am. The case was listed with all the others and treated like all the others, lumped in, as though there were no difference, with abandoned cars, forged ten pound notes, drunk and disorderly behaviour and attempts by financial houses to recover debts owing to them.

The child, her estranged parents, her disputatious grandparents, her aunts and uncles, and their children, her social workers and doctors, nineteen in all, milled about the dreary, dark, dirty, narrow corridor in various combinations of silence and spoken hostilities. One of them would occasionally step out into the rain for fresh air, and come back soaked.

It is as yet beyond the competence of court officials to anticipate that the custody case of a child will involve many people and much time, and that a special fixed time and place should be set aside for them. In this particular instance, the courtesy of the public waiting room was not afforded them. That private place was for solicitors and their clients, and their solicitors were inside before the justice, engaged on other business.

So the people involved waited and waited and waited, and you could see that any one of them could have done with a cup of tea, perhaps even a glass of milk for any of the children, but they dared not leave the corridor lest the case be called.

It was called, finally, after one o'clock. The Justice looked at the summons sheet, looked at the clock, looked at the parties ranged before him and announced that it was too serious a matter to be dealt with quickly. He would hear it after lunch, beginning promptly, he said, at ten minutes past two. Lunch costs money when you're far from home, and tempers can fray when you've been at court since breakfast time with young children, and it's raining outside, and you've just been told to go away and come back, but away they all went and back they all came, promptly, just before ten past.

The court doors were locked. The people stood in the roadway until twenty past. Then they stood in court, on their feet, obliged to stand on their feet until the Justice should have seated himself, which he did, and then the seated parties heard that the Justice would hear a few other matters before dealing with them. Policemen in a hurry were accommodated.

The people filed out to the corridor. Tension rose in the corridor because one of these people, a male relation of the mother, was suspected of the child abuse, and he hadn't been charged, had he, the police had brought him to the station only the night before for questioning and they had no evidence, had they, so he was innocent, wasn't he?

These things he said in the corridor, and those who suspected him said nothing, because he hadn't been charged, and was not the subject of the summons. The mother of the child was. She had been summonsed, because she had not heeded the suspicions about him, and here the man was, demanding that she stand by him.

They filed into court at twenty minutes to three and the solicitor representing the Health Board asked the Justice to exclude members of the public. Some of the details of abuse were explicit, he said, and the witnesses might be embarrassed if strangers were present.

The Justice refused to exclude anybody. He might ask people to leave during the case, depending on the detail, he said, but not for the moment. The solicitor forgot to ask that the names of all parties concerned be kept private. The Justice forgot to request this of the press.

The hearing lasted two hours, and the man who was not summonsed for child abuse was named by a doctor from the Sexual Assault Unit at the Rotunda Hospital. The child had been given dolls to play with, named after her relatives, and had refused to play with the doll named after this man. The child had given the doctor explicit details of what this man had done to her.

While these details were being given the child was outside the court. So was the man. They were outside in the corridor together. He hadn't been summonsed, had he? Occasionally he banged into the courtroom, letting the slam of the door proclaim his unsummonsed innocence.

There was a conflict of evidence between the mother and her social worker. The social worker had gathered from hints and stories over the years that the man was not to be trusted with children. The mother said she had not understood the hints.

The man hadn't been summonsed, had he? He still wasn't, was he? Matters might not have come to a head, indeed, if the grandmother of the child had not recently noticed bruised vaginal tissue. It was the grandmother who sent for a doctor, not the social worker. It was after the grandmother had set events in train that the social workers had moved to take the child out of the mother's home. . .

After the revelations by newspapers, after the *Women's Programme,* after the *Today Tonight* special, after the setting up of the Sexual Assault Unit . . . after everybody had learned to cope in a situation where you still couldn't summons the man.

The mother who was summonsed revealed her bewilderment, ignorance and confusion about the newly recognised phenomenon. 'The doctor didn't say she was raped, did she? Did she?' Slowly she accepted that her male relative had abused the child; that abuse does not solely consist of rape. 'Well, I don't know . . . if the doctor says so . . . she might have been . . . she must have been.'

The man continued to bang in and out of the courtroom, defiant in the absence of a summons. The Justice announced at half past four that he would have to think about the matter overnight.

Next day the mother's name was in the papers, but not that of the man. She had been summonsed, he had not. The people all trooped back into court. They had to wait while other cases were heard. At eleven am the Justice gave his verdict. The child should stay with its paternal grandparents for four months until the mother had a chance to 'prove herself'.

Irish Press, 12 December 1985.

Mary Norris

The country was shocked in July 1987, by the death of Mary Norris and her four daughters in a fire at their home in Clondalkin. Nell Mc-Cafferty had spoken to her weeks before after another fire there. Then she met a tiny, thin, wise-cracking woman who lived always on the edge of disaster. Mary Norris lost out to fate even earlier than her friends expected. Nell McCafferty tells her story.

Four weeks before her life ended, Mary Norris told me that she would welcome death. In the month succeeding that interview, those who knew her, neighbours, welfare officers and community workers alike, sensed that another disaster was approaching. They did not anticipate death, or the deaths of her four daughters.

Now that it has happened, they acknowledge, bleakly, that the circumstances of Mary's life were such that death must have seemed a release to her. She fell all the way through the welfare net. Try though they might, and many tried to help her, no one knew how. Mary moved like quicksilver on shifting sand.

At the heart's core of this wise-cracking, resourceful, childlike, childish, illiterate 29-year-old woman was loneliness. 'The only good thing to come out of me disasters is that the neighbours come round. I like that. I like the company,' she told me.

She was, at the time, sitting at her kitchen table, talking about yet another fire in her house. While she spoke, the women were making tea, bringing in clothes collected in the area to replace those burned, sweeping up debris, washing down the sooty walls. All the electricity in the house had been switched off as a safety precaution, save that in the kitchen which Corporation workmen left functioning. Her husband, Jamesy, was up in Finche's pub.

Mary hoped the *Irish Press* would publicise her story and help her secure a bigger, brand-new house around the corner. The damage to her livingroom did not justify such a move. A coat of paint, and fresh wallpaper, and re-wiring would have left the house as habitable as it was before, though as empty as before. The furnishings were meagre. The torn wallpaper in the bedrooms and hallway had been like that before the fire of June 10, which caused the neighbours to contact this newspaper.

Another new house, another new start, would only have provided another setting for the disasters that regularly engulfed Mary's life. House fires had already occurred in her previous Corporation homes in Blanchardstown and Ballyfermot. They were all small, all relatively non-threatening – the family had always survived.

Each time they moved, they moved onto another welfare file and another police file, bringing their innocuous catalogue of inadequacy along with them – an unemployed husband who drinks, a wife who took small overdoses of valium, children who attended special schools, a barring order against Jamesy, a small succession of dodgy welfare claims which were found out, a weekly appeal for Supplementary Welfare from the local Health Centre – just another poor family in a country where one-third of the population is living on the poverty line.

It was not expected that Mary would actually die under the burden of it all. The Church of the Immaculate Heart of Mary, where eight priests concelebrated Mass over the dead bodies of Mary Norris and her daughters, Catherine, Sabrina, Fiona and Deirdre, and consoled her neighbours with the announcement that all five of God's adopted daughters had surely entered Heaven, is placarded with appeals to look for help before it is too late.

The placards, stretching from floor to ceiling of the church, capture the problems of, and pitiful end-of-the-line resources available to, those members of the working-class who have been brought to their knees by deprivation. Like advertising hoardings, they proclaim that Talbot House is there to help drug addicts, Madonna House is a holding centre for children in need of care, Stewart's Hospital school will attend to slow learners of any age, a senior citizen block of flats will cater for the abandoned elderly, and CURA will help those with troubled pregnancies.

One placard announces that the Little Sisters of the Assumption have moved into Clondalkin. Their house is ten yards away from the one where Mary lived, Among the objectives of the nuns, the placard firmly declares, is the development of women. The Sisters believe that women hold the key to the regeneration of the area, and hold the fort against doom.

Mary used some of the resources advertised by the Church and devised many of her own. Her life was a catalogue of hard work, its sole end the procurement of the one thing that she could understand very well, which was money. Much of that went on Jamesy, and the rest on rent, fuel and food for the children. For herself, she demanded only cigarettes. The things that money could not buy, such as parenting skills, affection, literacy and financial management were beyond her reach.

A community worker recalls talking with Mary about food. She suggested that instead of tinned steak and kidney pie and bottles of lemonade, Mary should shop for other things. The community worker offered to accompany Mary to the supermarket to do a week's shopping.

Mary agreed, then took to her bed, saying she couldn't face it. The worker spent Mary's money for her, bringing back a bag of potatoes, mince, eggs and vegetables. 'Look, Mary, that will keep you for a week.' Two days later, Mary landed round in the welfare office to cadge some supplementary benefit.

'The kids don't like that kind of food. I have to buy the old stuff,' she said. The nuns enrolled Mary in their housekeeping classes. One of Mary's closest friends, who marvels now at how much she herself managed to save, and how her children's health improved, through what she learned from the nuns, remembers Mary's attendance at the kitchen-school.

'She loved being among the women. She kept us all in stitches with her jokes and her stories. She disrupted us entirely, then she dropped out. She said she preferred to eat the tinned foods.'

Mary grew on people. The friend explained how neighbours constantly rallied to the woman who was always troubled. A lawyer whom Mary visited in the Law Library every fortnight remembers the first time he met her, in 1973. He worked then with the Free Legal Advice Centre, a group of voluntary legal students who helped people decode the welfare maze.

'Our office was in the Vincent de Paul building in the inner city. She came wandering in, on her rounds. She hoped her poor health would get her extra points, and persuade the Corpo to transfer the family out of a slum flat. Her marriage had only started. It was in trouble. She was tiny, and thin, and had a quirky humour. I took to her.'

Some time later, the lawyer came across Mary begging at the entrance to the Hibernian Hotel. He chatted with her, gave her money, and resumed the relationship. 'She'd come down to the Law Library once a fortnight, send for me, and I'd give her a cheque or cash. She always carried a letter I gave her authorising her to cash the cheque at my bank on the Green. Towards the end, we didn't talk much. She'd tell me stories. I'd half listen. She'd receive her money, which is really all she came in for.'

Neighbours know the lawyer's name, but don't know the name of another benefactor, who saw to it that Mary's ESB bills were presented to a certain bank and paid by that bank. Mary's excellent status with the ESB ensured that shortly before the fire in June she was able to buy a ghetto-blaster on credit from them.

Speaking amid the ashes of the June fire, Mary pointed to the transistor and said she had bought it for Catherine, to help the girl forget the fire that had engulfed Mary's mother's house. Catherine had been staying with her granny in Ballyfermot, when a blaze killed the granny and Catherine's uncle.

The gardai are satisfied that fire had nothing to do with the fires that regularly broke out in Mary's own homes. The death of her mother and brother was a separate end to a separate catalogue of disasters that had characterised Mary's pre-marriage life – and their brother serving fifteen years in Mountjoy, a third killed in Ballyfermot during gang warfare between petty thieves, an uncle serving life in England.

Mary's mother was of travelling people stock, who married and settled down with a local man. Her friends remember Mary at fifteen selling paper roses in Ballyfermot. By sixteen she was pregnant, then married.

She stayed close to her parents, regularly going to chat with them. She would see her mother several times a week. After her mother burned to death on April 16, Mary was plunged into grief. An intimate conversational outlet had been destroyed. 'She loved to talk. She came down here every Monday looking for money, but you knew perfectly well that she really wanted a conversation. She was lonely,' says a member of the Rowlagh Health Centre.

She always brought some of her children with her. Sometimes she left them behind in the Health Centre, saying she wanted them taken into care, as she often brought them to hospital saying the same thing, but then she frequently adopted a similar attitude to Jamesy.

One day she wanted rid of him, the next she wanted to stay with him. After a few hours in the Health Centre, the social worker would bring the children back to Mary's house, a few steps away. Mary would ask if the children had been given their dinner, and if they had, she would grin with delight. She had seen to it that her children were fed, one way or another, another small victory to chalk up against the failure of her mothering skills, which the cot death of her baby Shirley, years ago, seemed to represent to her.

She took her own steps against Jamesy, obtaining a court order barring him from the house on the grounds of assault. He wandered on back home anyway. Sometimes, when it got too much, she telephoned the guards from a neighbour's house. She informed them anonymously that it would be worth their while to check the Norris home for stolen goods. They might lift Jamesy and take him away for a while, she explained to her neighbour. This scheme backfired once when the guards removed the family television set, a massive brand new thing.

It took her days, with receipt and a completely accurate description of the shop where she bought it, to get it back.

There was one seeming scam, which preceded the three fires this year in Liscarne Gardens, which was not her fault, the neighbours swear. Mary had arranged years ago that social welfare payments be made out separately for her and Jamesy. He got £36 a week for himself; she got £74.35 for herself and the six children. Because she was illiterate, the neighbours filled out the necessary forms for her, every year, declaring the circumstances.

The separate payments were understood by the Corporation to indicate that Jamesy did not live with her, and her rent was adjusted to fifty pence a week. Then last October, when the new four-bedroomed houses went up, a neighbour suggested that Mary apply for one. It was near, she'd still have the company of friends she had built up, and there'd be more room for the couple, the four growing daughters and the two sons.

The neighbours helped her fill out the form. Someone in the Corpo noticed that the form showed that Jamesy lived with her, despite the separate payments, and an official landed round to announce that Mary's rent would go up to £15 a week, including back payments. That was a massive sum out of her £74, and a dreadful punishment, the neighbours felt, given that Mary had never handled the forms and had been truthful.

It meant that Mary had to work even harder to supply her

family's needs. Shortly after that, the first fire occurred, then the one that might justify a newspaper plea for re-housing, then the one that killed Mary and the four girls. Re-housing might have meant new forms, and a Corpo official who was not entirely alert, and perhaps a restoration of low rent to Mary and Jamesy – these are the things neighbours wonder about as they look back over Mary's life and scams, and Jamesy's peripatetic life around the Corporation houses of Dublin.

Mary's hard work included petty shop-lifting. The Judges always let her go after hearing her stories. The last conviction, she told me, was for stealing a pair of black slacks which she needed to wear to her mother's funeral. Under gentle nudging of her memory by a neighbour, Mary realised that she had stolen the trousers before her mother's death.

That she needed clothes, there is no doubt. Her money always went on the others, particularly to Jamesy. Sometimes, when the women decided to go to Finche's for a celebration of their own, Mary would wear Catherine's Confirmation outfit. She was so thin and small, the child's clothes fitted her perfectly.

She was so thin that the Health Centre allowed a special payment of £10 a week for a dietary supplement for her alone. It was not felt, however, that she would spend the money on herself. An arrangement was made with a supermarket that the cheque supplied to Jamesy would be spent only on good food for Mary.

Jamesy had been used to making his own arrangements for what he considered were his and Mary's needs in Finche's pub. He asked there that she not be allowed in before ten o'clock at night, and then only if he were in the pub himself. In the last week of Mary's life, Jamesy's request was made redundant. Mary was barred by management from going in there without him around, because in the days before her death she had taken to going round the pub collecting money to replace the furniture damaged in the June fire. She concentrated on customers who, she deluded herself, did not know her. Mary was tirelessly and anonymously organising a benefit collection for her own family. It was foolish but it was funny, and neighbours cheered her ingenuity.

She didn't often go to Finche's, but when she did she amused her friends by her antics in getting round Jamesy's pub decree. She would drop to her hands and knees and secure a table out of his sight. The Finche's is a vast, darkened place, with two small windows paying perfunctory lip-service to the world beyond the public bar. Under its electric light, and with the television flickering steadily in the background, it is impossible to tell day from night.

Men who have not been able to get work, to whom day and night are as one long nightmare, crowd into it from the moment it opens. There are no self-help classes for the unemployed men of Clondalkin. The meagre voluntary and state resources are aimed at women who keep the family's body and soul together.

The men who do stay at home get under their women's feet. There is unconcealed irritation at the traditionally unnatural crowding together, during working hours, of a husband and wife and adult children as well, in a house where there is no hope that jobs will one day come.

Living on the edges of society, Mary had no hope, but a gift for cheering other women up. She would suggest an evening in the pub, and then, as one of her friends put it, 'I will never forget what she did for me. All my life I only ever had birthday cards from my family – from brothers and sisters, and parents, and my husband. One night in the pub, the lights went out, and a barman appeared with a cake lit with candles, and Mary started singing Happy Birthday. She had arranged the whole thing. She took me out of my world, do you know what I mean, and brought me into a public one. For the first time in my life, other people knew it was the anniversary of the day I was born.'

None of the women for whom she arranged these treats minded at all when Mary called around next day and borrowed money to keep her going. She was scrupulously careful to repay her debts to her neighbours, in feast and famine. She often lent them money herself.

Her children sensed that begging and repaying was a way of communication. The night of the final fire, Fiona and Deirdre had gone up and down the road borrowing tea bags. A neighbour decided to call in and see if Mary was in a food-crisis. There were plenty of tea bags and need of none. The children's allowance money had been paid out only that day, and Jamesy had given her some of it.

Mary and the neighbour burst out laughing, and went on to celebrate Mary's latest stroke of luck – the suite which had replaced the one burned in June, thanks to donations from the *Gay*

Byrne Show and a welfare supplement, was installed in the repaired livingroom, and only that night a second suite had been delivered to Mary's door.

The neighbour did not question its provenance, because Mary had so many stories to explain things. Instead, she sat on this second suite in the kitchen, marvelling at it. It might or might not, she knew, be sold out the back door, as Mary was often wont to do when a deluge of luck came her way.

The kitchen suite, where before there had only been a humble table and chair, added to the kitchen fire and smoke that killed Mary and her daughters hours later as they slept.

Mary, modest in the extreme, had worried about her daughters. When she discovered Catherine bleeding before the age of ten, she consulted the other women about the early arrival of menstruation. The women spoke with Catherine, and Catherine talked of a man in a van who had offered her lollipops and touched her. There had been no menstruation. The neighbours advised Mary to take Catherine to hospital. Mary said later that one hospital talked of sexual interference, another had dismissed the notion. The gardai are checking out Mary's story now.

They have also interviewed the neighbour to whom Mary turned last year when she thought that a strange smell and substance seeped from Fiona's little genital area.

This neighbour looked at Fiona, then aged six, and said her genitals were raw and distorted and swollen and bore no visible relationship to the rawness that occurs regularly in little children who wet their pants, or are not regularly bathed. In any case, Mary kept a spotless house, and turned her children out beautifully.

This neighbour advised hospital again. The gardai are checking hospital records. Neighbours, drawing on their deepest, most affectionate resources, could not adequately cope with Mary's worries about her two girls. The Church has no placard drawing attention to this latest crisis of which Ireland is becoming painfully aware.

A Community worker to whom Mary sent Catherine for sex education wonders in retrospect, now, if Mary was sending out yet another signal for help. So many signals, so many small signals, so many conflicting stories from Mary, who did the very best she could, scrabbling for money for her family, while living an outwardly laughing life of the deepest loneliness and despair. She married young, she died young, she never had the leisure or opportunity to grow up. Since becoming a child-bride, she was preoccupied with being a mother.

It's hard enough being a mother, if you know how to be, and have a partner who knows how to be a father, and both have the time and maturity and freedom from financial woe to acquire the skills. Love is not always sufficient, although among the very poorest love is all they have to offer.

Social workers are reluctant in the extreme to remove children from their parents, especially given the miserly alternative in this country to a family home. In the vast area where Mary lived, in any case, called Area Five in Eastern Health Board parlance, cut-backs have reduced the number of social workers from five to one solitary overworked individual. This person had not the time to call on Mary between the second fire and the third one which killed her.

A voluntary worker, who discussed the plight of the Norris family after Mary had spoken with me, offered a consolation born out of experience in an area deluged with deprivation. 'Children can survive anything,' she said.

The four Norris girls did not.

For Catherine (12), Sabrina (8), Fiona (7) and Deirdre (3), there was no more salvation than there was for Mary, their mother.

Irish Press, 6 July 1987.

Mary's husband James Norris has been charged with her murder. The case is pending.

Santa and the Tomboy

Santa once made a mistake. My mother explained to me that he had an awful lot of work to do, delivering toys to every child in Derry. She asked me to forgive him. I could not. I was inconsolable.

I had, after all, behaved as well as every child in the street. When George the postman stood at the foot of the hill, his sack bulging, dreading the long climb up, I had queued to help him. I delivered the cards as dutifully as any other. When Harry the milkman swung over the brow, pleading with his horse to hold still a minute, I did not frighten the animal. The bottles were cold in winter, and if you dropped one you'd be killed, but I helped Harry do his job, just like any other child.

The pudding was hard to mix, and raisins were expensive, and I understood it was a venial sin to eat any, and I committed no sin. I mixed with the best of them. I went to the snug in the pub for the little bottle of brandy, and kept my lips shut, as instructed, as to the names of the women I saw there.

I had paid a portion of my pocket money every week into the corner shop, as a deposit on the Christmas comic annual. I knew, because my father had explained to me, that Santa couldn't pay for everything, and children had to help him out.

I had gone to church, to confession, and I did not climb over the altar rails to lie down in the straw of the crib. I prayed for the baby Jesus, that he would have a Happy Christmas too and I thanked God that I was born in a house, instead of a stable.

I wrote my note to Santa in my very best handwriting, and made sure it went right up the chimney and was not burned in the flames. I brushed my teeth, did not cry when my mother drew a fine comb through my curls, and fell asleep as fast as I could. I did not call out from bedroom to bedroom to Muireanna, Nuala, Hugh, Paddy or Carmel.

If anything, I was asleep before they were, because I was a very good child indeed.

So where did I go wrong, I asked my parents as dawn broke over the rooftops, and the others laughed with glee, pointing out the treasures Santa had brought them. My own present had left me silent and horror struck. Perhaps Santa made a mistake, said one parent. Perhaps Santa thought this present would suit me better, said another.

I cried all the way to early morning Mass.

I wandered from altar to altar, there being three in the church. There were three masses going on at once. I went to every one of them, praying to the baby Jesus to help me, praying for Santa to come back.

In mid-morning my mother said he wasn't coming back, and suggested I go out to the street to join the other children. She made me take my present with me. Any hope she had that the other children would envy my good luck disappeared when she saw how they shunned me. It broke her heart she says now, looking back over the years. I was, she said, like little orphan Annie, walking up and down on my own.

All around me was frolic and joy, as girls and boys formed themselves into gangs of cowboys and Indians. Roy Rogers, Calamity Jane, and Geronimo were the heroes that year. I was affronted, so I was, pushing a pram with a doll in it. I was shot so often, with bullets and arrows, it's a wonder I came back home alive.

My own father passed me by in silence. He tried to sneak around the corner, on his way to God-knows-where, and tried to sneak back. I saw him on his return journey. Why wouldn't I, since I too was hiding in the lane, seeking shelter in the lee of our back-yard door.

When I was finally called in for dinner, Mammy said Santa was in a terrible state. Santa thought that I was a big girl of nine. He didn't realise that I was only eight and still a tomboy. He hoped I would forgive him, and he had left me the six-gun I asked for. I turned the pram into a wagon, and defended my doll against every Indian in Beechwood Street.

Sure I knew rightly that Santa couldn't let me down.

Kerry's Eye, December 1986.

Happy Christmas to every child in Kerry.

Family, family, family

There's no point in putting a gloss on it. Christmas ranks as the loneliest day in the year for the person who is gay, unknown to the rest of the family. All over the western world on the 25th December, hearts will beat homeward, to the mammy, and the daddy. Homage will be paid, extracted, volunteered and involuntarily wrung from the withers.

It is culturally irresistible. It has been bred into us. It has given us some of the happiest moments in our lives, has Christmas Day, and the memory lingers on, stirred by the pealing carols, the bright shop fronts, the hint of frost, the smell of turkey and pudding. 'I'm dreaming of . . .' we'll hum at the bus stop, and 'Silent night, holy night, all is calm, all is bright' we'll sing in the pubs and the factories and the offices, as the moment draws near, because they're both grand songs and who could stand aside from the impulse to joy and good cheer that will pervade the meanest group amongst us.

And then will come the day, the one day of the year, when we're all obliged to play at happy families, and will seize the chance to do so, because the family was happy once; when we were children, and who among us would begrudge the pretence that it is still so, would burst the bubble and shout 'Mammy, Daddy, I left my childhood behind years ago'.

So in we will all troop, the daughters and sons and our spouses and our children, and those of us with neither spouse nor child, but lover left behind in another townland, and those of us with neither spouse nor child nor lover, glad to get in out of the cold. And our mothers and fathers will watch and wonder and wait and pray that not today, not today baby Jesus, will the family front be breached. They know, of course they know, that for the other 364 days of the year, their children are not what they seem to be; parents did not come down in the last shower; the relationship has not been thought nor wrought that is unknown to them, but that does not mean that words have to be put on these things, they may never have put words on these things, but they know; it's just that one day a year they prefer not to know, as we prefer not to remember, that once there were shouts in this house, and tears and cruel words.

That's life.

The 25th is not a day for life; it is a day for impossible dreams. It is a day for the most impossible dream of it all – that Jesus, Mary and Joseph were a normal unit. Impregnated by a ghost, what? pregnant outside marriage in the eyes of her community, what? gave birth in a stable among the animals, what? never slept with her elderly husband, not once, what?

Put like that, and taken in the context of her time, two thousand years ago, when women were stoned to death for adultery, nobody believed in ghosts, and the unmarried mother of any Kerry baby would never have survived as far as the courts, there is some comfort for the gay person. Mary had it rough too. A lesser woman lying on straw, would have told the three Wise Holy Men, bearing baubles, to fuck away off.

She didn't and we won't. Not on Christmas Day. We'll stay away or we'll keep quiet. There are 364 other days in which to win friends and enemies to a redefined notion of family; on this one day the mammy and the daddy would like a rest; Jaysus, they're entitled to it, sure they never meant us any harm; they only ever wished the best for us.

Happy, happy Christmas, sisters and brothers. Goodnight Jesus, goodnight Mary, goodnight Joseph. Who're ye tellin?

Out Magazine, June 1986.

Near Relations

Produced, written and directed by Nell McCafferty and starring Shirley MacLaine, Princess Margaret, Jacqueline Onassis Kennedy, Nell's sister Muireanna and her husband Maurice, Rod Steiger, the Provos, the Buncrana tourist industry and Roddy Llewellyn.

Marriage is getting a bad name. That is not good. Marriage is not necessarily bad for everyone. For example, it is because of marriage that I am nearly related to Jacqueline Kennedy Onassis and Princess Margaret of England. With credentials like that I expect to prosper.

Let me explain.

In 1968 an American journalist called Pete Hamill came to Derry to cover the riots. We met. Over the years we became friendly. One year he brought his brother along. His brother met my sister Carmel. They became . . . quite . . . friendly. Pete's brother pondered marriage with my sister. She pondered too, albeit briefly.

Peter went away and the next thing we heard he was going out with Shirley MacLaine. The thought of connections with Hollywood inspired my family to urge my sister to ponder quickly and positively. She could be the sister-in-law of Shirley MacLaine's husband Pete. That would make the rest of us somebodies.

'We could be somebodies', we twanged in Rod Steiger tones to Carmel, as we walked her up and down what was left of Derry's waterfront.

Shirley and Pete broke up.

We decided our sister shouldn't be rushed into marriage with just anybody, and brought her home off the waterfront. Pete then started going out with Jacqueline Kennedy Onassis. It was too exquisitely delicious to bear. If Peter married Jackie, and Carmel married Pete's brother, we'd be spending our summers on Cape Cod, or wherever Jackie goes for holiday, who's fussy?

Of course, we'd have to repaper the back bedroom of our family home, not just because she was an Onassis but because that's the kind of thing you do when welcoming the wife of your sister's brother-in-law into your home for the first time.

Pete and Jackie broke up.

By now, my sister couldn't remember Pete's brother's name.

Around the same period, my sister Muireanna was prospering with her husband Maurice in London. Maurice was a Buncrana, Co. Donegal, man. Buncrana men stick together wherever they go, and Maurice's best friend was doing well in London too. So well, in fact, that he opened a restaurant cum pub, called a brasserie these days, I do believe.

This best friend hired Roddy Llewellyn to front his brasserie. Roddy knew lots of London people. In particular, he knew Princess Margaret very well. There was talk of romance. My sister Muireanna and her husband Maurice were invited to the opening of Maurice's best friend's brasserie, to which Roddy was expected to invite Princess Margaret. Our family telephoned Muireanna a list of questions that she was to put to Margaret (for such we called her now), and not to forget particularly to ask if it was true that the Queen Mother kept a naggin of gin always in her handbag.

The family home in Derry was critically scrutinised. Could we rise to another repapering of the back bedroom? Would the Provos picket the place if they heard the Queen was staying with us? Bloody Provos. They spoil a person's marriage prospects something shocking. There was no question of bringing the Queen, Margaret and Roddy to Buncrana for the day. Buncrana people would rob you with their prices. Everything is doubled when they see a tourist coming.

Anyway, on the night, Roddy turned up and announced that he and Margaret had broken it off. Naturally Roddy was sacked. He's a gardener now.

I don't know why people think marriage is boring.

It's full of prospects.

In Dublin, 1 November 1982.

A selection of books by Nell McCafferty

NELL McCAFFERTY is "an original. She is one of those few lucky people that must be loved or hated, because she has a magnetic pull that polarises energy." *Irish Press*

THE BEST OF NELL:
A Selection of Writings over 14 Years
"More than the best in Irish Journalism, it is a unique account of modern Irish life." *New Hibernia*
1 946211 051 £10.00 (hb)
1 946211 06X £4.99 / $9.99 (pb)

A WOMAN TO BLAME:
The Kerry Babies Case
"An important and disturbing document ... she is a trenchant writer and her treatment of some of the evidence can only be described as an indictment." *The Irish Times*
1 946211 221 £10.00 (hb)
1 946211 213 £3.95 / $7.95 (pb)

PEGGY DEERY:
A Derry Family at War
This is the extraordinary story of an ordinary mother. Peggy Deery's life, scarred with tragedy, traces the story of the northern troubles and the way people, particularly women, have withstood the wars northern society has waged on them.
1 946211 566 £10.00 (hb)
1 946211 558 £4.95 (pb)

NELL McCAFFERTY & PAT MURPHY

WOMEN IN FOCUS:
Contemporary Irish Women's Lives
"Captures in a series of stunning photographs the plural realities of Irish women's everyday lives." *Women's Review of Books*
1 946211 310 £19.95 (hb)
302 £9.95 / $19.95 (pb)